C-3991   CAREER EXAMINATION SERIES

This is your
PASSBOOK for...

Assistant Conductor

Test Preparation Study Guide
Questions & Answers

NATIONAL LEARNING CORPORATION®

COPYRIGHT NOTICE

This book is SOLELY intended for, is sold ONLY to, and its use is RESTRICTED to individual, bona fide applicants or candidates who qualify by virtue of having seriously filed applications for appropriate license, certificate, professional and/or promotional advancement, higher school matriculation, scholarship, or other legitimate requirements of education and/or governmental authorities.

This book is NOT intended for use, class instruction, tutoring, training, duplication, copying, reprinting, excerption, or adaptation, etc., by:

1) Other publishers
2) Proprietors and/or Instructors of "Coaching" and/or Preparatory Courses
3) Personnel and/or Training Divisions of commercial, industrial, and governmental organizations
4) Schools, colleges, or universities and/or their departments and staffs, including teachers and other personnel
5) Testing Agencies or Bureaus
6) Study groups which seek by the purchase of a single volume to copy and/or duplicate and/or adapt this material for use by the group as a whole without having purchased individual volumes for each of the members of the group
7) Et al.

Such persons would be in violation of appropriate Federal and State statutes.

PROVISION OF LICENSING AGREEMENTS – Recognized educational, commercial, industrial, and governmental institutions and organizations, and others legitimately engaged in educational pursuits, including training, testing, and measurement activities, may address request for a licensing agreement to the copyright owners, who will determine whether, and under what conditions, including fees and charges, the materials in this book may be used them. In other words, a licensing facility exists for the legitimate use of the material in this book on other than an individual basis. However, it is asseverated and affirmed here that the material in this book CANNOT be used without the receipt of the express permission of such a licensing agreement from the Publishers. Inquiries re licensing should be addressed to the company, attention rights and permissions department.

All rights reserved, including the right of reproduction in whole or in part, in any form or by any means, electronic or mechanical, including photocopying, recording, or by any information storage and retrieval system, without permission in writing from the Publisher.

Copyright © 2025 by
National Learning Corporation

212 Michael Drive, Syosset, NY 11791
(516) 921-8888 • www.passbooks.com
E-mail: info@passbooks.com

PASSBOOK® SERIES

THE *PASSBOOK® SERIES* has been created to prepare applicants and candidates for the ultimate academic battlefield – the examination room.

At some time in our lives, each and every one of us may be required to take an examination – for validation, matriculation, admission, qualification, registration, certification, or licensure.

Based on the assumption that every applicant or candidate has met the basic formal educational standards, has taken the required number of courses, and read the necessary texts, the *PASSBOOK® SERIES* furnishes the one special preparation which may assure passing with confidence, instead of failing with insecurity. Examination questions – together with answers – are furnished as the basic vehicle for study so that the mysteries of the examination and its compounding difficulties may be eliminated or diminished by a sure method.

This book is meant to help you pass your examination provided that you qualify and are serious in your objective.

The entire field is reviewed through the huge store of content information which is succinctly presented through a provocative and challenging approach – the question-and-answer method.

A climate of success is established by furnishing the correct answers at the end of each test.

You soon learn to recognize types of questions, forms of questions, and patterns of questioning. You may even begin to anticipate expected outcomes.

You perceive that many questions are repeated or adapted so that you can gain acute insights, which may enable you to score many sure points.

You learn how to confront new questions, or types of questions, and to attack them confidently and work out the correct answers.

You note objectives and emphases, and recognize pitfalls and dangers, so that you may make positive educational adjustments.

Moreover, you are kept fully informed in relation to new concepts, methods, practices, and directions in the field.

You discover that you are actually taking the examination all the time: you are preparing for the examination by "taking" an examination, not by reading extraneous and/or supererogatory textbooks.

In short, this PASSBOOK®, used directedly, should be an important factor in helping you to pass your test.

ASSISTANT CONDUCTOR/TRAINEE

DUTIES
Provides excellent customer service to all passengers. Assists train crew in the safe and efficient movement of customers, performance of various yard movement operations, mechanical troubleshooting/minor repairs of equipment, collecting and selling cash fares, making announcements, operating doors, handling emergency situations, coupling and uncoupling train cars, throwing switches, etc.

RESPONSIBILITIES
Responsibilities may include but are not limited to:
- Provides passengers with information, answers questions concerning train rules, regulations, and schedules, and provides destination information. Reports delays.
- Inspects, collects, and sells cash fares on passenger trains in accordance with established procedures.
- Must walk through moving passenger trains in performance of duties, climb on and off equipment using fixed ladders or stairs, assist passengers on, off and through trains routinely or under emergency conditions.
- Routinely operates yard and main track switches and derails, operates levers and valves to separate cars, couples and uncouples air brake hoses, inspects trains, performs minor repairs to equipment, applies or releases hand brakes, aligns coupling assemblies, opens and closes doom on passenger equipment
- Assists in the movement of cars to assemble trains or place for repair or service.
- Observes, interprets, and relays various types of signals including hand, fixed position, or color lights to control the movement of trains and engines for the safety of passengers.
- Reads and understands rules and instructions, gives as well as follows written and oral instructions, communicates clearly via public address and radio systems with passengers and railroad facilities.
- Provides protection (flag) for third party contractors along tracks, on platforms, bridges, tunnels and other railroad facilities.

SCOPE OF THE EXAMINATION
The written test will be designed to test for knowledge, skills, and/or abilities in such areas as:
1. Cognitive;
2. Vocabulary; and
3. Mathematics.

HOW TO TAKE A TEST

I. YOU MUST PASS AN EXAMINATION

A. WHAT EVERY CANDIDATE SHOULD KNOW
Examination applicants often ask us for help in preparing for the written test. What can I study in advance? What kinds of questions will be asked? How will the test be given? How will the papers be graded?

As an applicant for a civil service examination, you may be wondering about some of these things. Our purpose here is to suggest effective methods of advance study and to describe civil service examinations.

Your chances for success on this examination can be increased if you know how to prepare. Those "pre-examination jitters" can be reduced if you know what to expect. You can even experience an adventure in good citizenship if you know why civil service exams are given.

B. WHY ARE CIVIL SERVICE EXAMINATIONS GIVEN?
Civil service examinations are important to you in two ways. As a citizen, you want public jobs filled by employees who know how to do their work. As a job seeker, you want a fair chance to compete for that job on an equal footing with other candidates. The best-known means of accomplishing this two-fold goal is the competitive examination.

Exams are widely publicized throughout the nation. They may be administered for jobs in federal, state, city, municipal, town or village governments or agencies.

Any citizen may apply, with some limitations, such as the age or residence of applicants. Your experience and education may be reviewed to see whether you meet the requirements for the particular examination. When these requirements exist, they are reasonable and applied consistently to all applicants. Thus, a competitive examination may cause you some uneasiness now, but it is your privilege and safeguard.

C. HOW ARE CIVIL SERVICE EXAMS DEVELOPED?
Examinations are carefully written by trained technicians who are specialists in the field known as "psychological measurement," in consultation with recognized authorities in the field of work that the test will cover. These experts recommend the subject matter areas or skills to be tested; only those knowledges or skills important to your success on the job are included. The most reliable books and source materials available are used as references. Together, the experts and technicians judge the difficulty level of the questions.

Test technicians know how to phrase questions so that the problem is clearly stated. Their ethics do not permit "trick" or "catch" questions. Questions may have been tried out on sample groups, or subjected to statistical analysis, to determine their usefulness.

Written tests are often used in combination with performance tests, ratings of training and experience, and oral interviews. All of these measures combine to form the best-known means of finding the right person for the right job.

II. HOW TO PASS THE WRITTEN TEST

A. NATURE OF THE EXAMINATION

To prepare intelligently for civil service examinations, you should know how they differ from school examinations you have taken. In school you were assigned certain definite pages to read or subjects to cover. The examination questions were quite detailed and usually emphasized memory. Civil service exams, on the other hand, try to discover your present ability to perform the duties of a position, plus your potentiality to learn these duties. In other words, a civil service exam attempts to predict how successful you will be. Questions cover such a broad area that they cannot be as minute and detailed as school exam questions.

In the public service similar kinds of work, or positions, are grouped together in one "class." This process is known as *position-classification*. All the positions in a class are paid according to the salary range for that class. One class title covers all of these positions, and they are all tested by the same examination.

B. FOUR BASIC STEPS

1) Study the announcement

How, then, can you know what subjects to study? Our best answer is: "Learn as much as possible about the class of positions for which you've applied." The exam will test the knowledge, skills and abilities needed to do the work.

Your most valuable source of information about the position you want is the official exam announcement. This announcement lists the training and experience qualifications. Check these standards and apply only if you come reasonably close to meeting them.

The brief description of the position in the examination announcement offers some clues to the subjects which will be tested. Think about the job itself. Review the duties in your mind. Can you perform them, or are there some in which you are rusty? Fill in the blank spots in your preparation.

Many jurisdictions preview the written test in the exam announcement by including a section called "Knowledge and Abilities Required," "Scope of the Examination," or some similar heading. Here you will find out specifically what fields will be tested.

2) Review your own background

Once you learn in general what the position is all about, and what you need to know to do the work, ask yourself which subjects you already know fairly well and which need improvement. You may wonder whether to concentrate on improving your strong areas or on building some background in your fields of weakness. When the announcement has specified "some knowledge" or "considerable knowledge," or has used adjectives like "beginning principles of…" or "advanced … methods," you can get a clue as to the number and difficulty of questions to be asked in any given field. More questions, and hence broader coverage, would be included for those subjects which are more important in the work. Now weigh your strengths and weaknesses against the job requirements and prepare accordingly.

3) Determine the level of the position

Another way to tell how intensively you should prepare is to understand the level of the job for which you are applying. Is it the entering level? In other words, is this the position in which beginners in a field of work are hired? Or is it an intermediate or advanced level? Sometimes this is indicated by such words as "Junior" or "Senior" in the class title. Other jurisdictions use Roman numerals to designate the level – Clerk I, Clerk II, for example. The word "Supervisor" sometimes appears in the title. If the level is not indicated by the title, check the description of duties. Will you be working under very close supervision, or will you have responsibility for independent decisions in this work?

4) Choose appropriate study materials

Now that you know the subjects to be examined and the relative amount of each subject to be covered, you can choose suitable study materials. For beginning level jobs, or even advanced ones, if you have a pronounced weakness in some aspect of your training, read a modern, standard textbook in that field. Be sure it is up to date and has general coverage. Such books are normally available at your library, and the librarian will be glad to help you locate one. For entry-level positions, questions of appropriate difficulty are chosen – neither highly advanced questions, nor those too simple. Such questions require careful thought but not advanced training.

If the position for which you are applying is technical or advanced, you will read more advanced, specialized material. If you are already familiar with the basic principles of your field, elementary textbooks would waste your time. Concentrate on advanced textbooks and technical periodicals. Think through the concepts and review difficult problems in your field.

These are all general sources. You can get more ideas on your own initiative, following these leads. For example, training manuals and publications of the government agency which employs workers in your field can be useful, particularly for technical and professional positions. A letter or visit to the government department involved may result in more specific study suggestions, and certainly will provide you with a more definite idea of the exact nature of the position you are seeking.

III. KINDS OF TESTS

Tests are used for purposes other than measuring knowledge and ability to perform specified duties. For some positions, it is equally important to test ability to make adjustments to new situations or to profit from training. In others, basic mental abilities not dependent on information are essential. Questions which test these things may not appear as pertinent to the duties of the position as those which test for knowledge and information. Yet they are often highly important parts of a fair examination. For very general questions, it is almost impossible to help you direct your study efforts. What we can do is to point out some of the more common of these general abilities needed in public service positions and describe some typical questions.

1) General information

Broad, general information has been found useful for predicting job success in some kinds of work. This is tested in a variety of ways, from vocabulary lists to questions about current events. Basic background in some field of work, such as sociology or economics, may be sampled in a group of questions. Often these are principles which have become familiar to most persons through exposure rather than through formal training. It is difficult to advise you how to study for these questions; being alert to the world around you is our best suggestion.

2) Verbal ability

An example of an ability needed in many positions is verbal or language ability. Verbal ability is, in brief, the ability to use and understand words. Vocabulary and grammar tests are typical measures of this ability. Reading comprehension or paragraph interpretation questions are common in many kinds of civil service tests. You are given a paragraph of written material and asked to find its central meaning.

3) Numerical ability
Number skills can be tested by the familiar arithmetic problem, by checking paired lists of numbers to see which are alike and which are different, or by interpreting charts and graphs. In the latter test, a graph may be printed in the test booklet which you are asked to use as the basis for answering questions.

4) Observation
A popular test for law-enforcement positions is the observation test. A picture is shown to you for several minutes, then taken away. Questions about the picture test your ability to observe both details and larger elements.

5) Following directions
In many positions in the public service, the employee must be able to carry out written instructions dependably and accurately. You may be given a chart with several columns, each column listing a variety of information. The questions require you to carry out directions involving the information given in the chart.

6) Skills and aptitudes
Performance tests effectively measure some manual skills and aptitudes. When the skill is one in which you are trained, such as typing or shorthand, you can practice. These tests are often very much like those given in business school or high school courses. For many of the other skills and aptitudes, however, no short-time preparation can be made. Skills and abilities natural to you or that you have developed throughout your lifetime are being tested.

Many of the general questions just described provide all the data needed to answer the questions and ask you to use your reasoning ability to find the answers. Your best preparation for these tests, as well as for tests of facts and ideas, is to be at your physical and mental best. You, no doubt, have your own methods of getting into an exam-taking mood and keeping "in shape." The next section lists some ideas on this subject.

IV. KINDS OF QUESTIONS

Only rarely is the "essay" question, which you answer in narrative form, used in civil service tests. Civil service tests are usually of the short-answer type. Full instructions for answering these questions will be given to you at the examination. But in case this is your first experience with short-answer questions and separate answer sheets, here is what you need to know:

1) Multiple-choice Questions
Most popular of the short-answer questions is the "multiple choice" or "best answer" question. It can be used, for example, to test for factual knowledge, ability to solve problems or judgment in meeting situations found at work.
A multiple-choice question is normally one of three types—
- It can begin with an incomplete statement followed by several possible endings. You are to find the one ending which *best* completes the statement, although some of the others may not be entirely wrong.
- It can also be a complete statement in the form of a question which is answered by choosing one of the statements listed.

- It can be in the form of a problem – again you select the best answer.

Here is an example of a multiple-choice question with a discussion which should give you some clues as to the method for choosing the right answer:

When an employee has a complaint about his assignment, the action which will *best* help him overcome his difficulty is to
   A. discuss his difficulty with his coworkers
   B. take the problem to the head of the organization
   C. take the problem to the person who gave him the assignment
   D. say nothing to anyone about his complaint

In answering this question, you should study each of the choices to find which is best. Consider choice "A" – Certainly an employee may discuss his complaint with fellow employees, but no change or improvement can result, and the complaint remains unresolved. Choice "B" is a poor choice since the head of the organization probably does not know what assignment you have been given, and taking your problem to him is known as "going over the head" of the supervisor. The supervisor, or person who made the assignment, is the person who can clarify it or correct any injustice. Choice "C" is, therefore, correct. To say nothing, as in choice "D," is unwise. Supervisors have and interest in knowing the problems employees are facing, and the employee is seeking a solution to his problem.

2) True/False Questions

The "true/false" or "right/wrong" form of question is sometimes used. Here a complete statement is given. Your job is to decide whether the statement is right or wrong.

SAMPLE: A roaming cell-phone call to a nearby city costs less than a non-roaming call to a distant city.

This statement is wrong, or false, since roaming calls are more expensive.

This is not a complete list of all possible question forms, although most of the others are variations of these common types. You will always get complete directions for answering questions. Be sure you understand *how* to mark your answers – ask questions until you do.

V. RECORDING YOUR ANSWERS

Computer terminals are used more and more today for many different kinds of exams.

For an examination with very few applicants, you may be told to record your answers in the test booklet itself. Separate answer sheets are much more common. If this separate answer sheet is to be scored by machine – and this is often the case – it is highly important that you mark your answers correctly in order to get credit.

An electronic scoring machine is often used in civil service offices because of the speed with which papers can be scored. Machine-scored answer sheets must be marked with a pencil, which will be given to you. This pencil has a high graphite content which responds to the electronic scoring machine. As a matter of fact, stray dots may register as answers, so do not let your pencil rest on the answer sheet while you are pondering the correct answer. Also, if your pencil lead breaks or is otherwise defective, ask for another.

Since the answer sheet will be dropped in a slot in the scoring machine, be careful not to bend the corners or get the paper crumpled.

The answer sheet normally has five vertical columns of numbers, with 30 numbers to a column. These numbers correspond to the question numbers in your test booklet. After each number, going across the page are four or five pairs of dotted lines. These short dotted lines have small letters or numbers above them. The first two pairs may also have a "T" or "F" above the letters. This indicates that the first two pairs only are to be used if the questions are of the true-false type. If the questions are multiple choice, disregard the "T" and "F" and pay attention only to the small letters or numbers.

Answer your questions in the manner of the sample that follows:

32. The largest city in the United States is
    A. Washington, D.C.
    B. New York City
    C. Chicago
    D. Detroit
    E. San Francisco

1) Choose the answer you think is best. (New York City is the largest, so "B" is correct.)
2) Find the row of dotted lines numbered the same as the question you are answering. (Find row number 32)
3) Find the pair of dotted lines corresponding to the answer. (Find the pair of lines under the mark "B.")
4) Make a solid black mark between the dotted lines.

VI. BEFORE THE TEST

Common sense will help you find procedures to follow to get ready for an examination. Too many of us, however, overlook these sensible measures. Indeed, nervousness and fatigue have been found to be the most serious reasons why applicants fail to do their best on civil service tests. Here is a list of reminders:

- Begin your preparation early – Don't wait until the last minute to go scurrying around for books and materials or to find out what the position is all about.
- Prepare continuously – An hour a night for a week is better than an all-night cram session. This has been definitely established. What is more, a night a week for a month will return better dividends than crowding your study into a shorter period of time.
- Locate the place of the exam – You have been sent a notice telling you when and where to report for the examination. If the location is in a different town or otherwise unfamiliar to you, it would be well to inquire the best route and learn something about the building.
- Relax the night before the test – Allow your mind to rest. Do not study at all that night. Plan some mild recreation or diversion; then go to bed early and get a good night's sleep.
- Get up early enough to make a leisurely trip to the place for the test – This way unforeseen events, traffic snarls, unfamiliar buildings, etc. will not upset you.
- Dress comfortably – A written test is not a fashion show. You will be known by number and not by name, so wear something comfortable.

- Leave excess paraphernalia at home – Shopping bags and odd bundles will get in your way. You need bring only the items mentioned in the official notice you received; usually everything you need is provided. Do not bring reference books to the exam. They will only confuse those last minutes and be taken away from you when in the test room.
- Arrive somewhat ahead of time – If because of transportation schedules you must get there very early, bring a newspaper or magazine to take your mind off yourself while waiting.
- Locate the examination room – When you have found the proper room, you will be directed to the seat or part of the room where you will sit. Sometimes you are given a sheet of instructions to read while you are waiting. Do not fill out any forms until you are told to do so; just read them and be prepared.
- Relax and prepare to listen to the instructions
- If you have any physical problem that may keep you from doing your best, be sure to tell the test administrator. If you are sick or in poor health, you really cannot do your best on the exam. You can come back and take the test some other time.

VII. AT THE TEST

The day of the test is here and you have the test booklet in your hand. The temptation to get going is very strong. Caution! There is more to success than knowing the right answers. You must know how to identify your papers and understand variations in the type of short-answer question used in this particular examination. Follow these suggestions for maximum results from your efforts:

1) Cooperate with the monitor

The test administrator has a duty to create a situation in which you can be as much at ease as possible. He will give instructions, tell you when to begin, check to see that you are marking your answer sheet correctly, and so on. He is not there to guard you, although he will see that your competitors do not take unfair advantage. He wants to help you do your best.

2) Listen to all instructions

Don't jump the gun! Wait until you understand all directions. In most civil service tests you get more time than you need to answer the questions. So don't be in a hurry. Read each word of instructions until you clearly understand the meaning. Study the examples, listen to all announcements and follow directions. Ask questions if you do not understand what to do.

3) Identify your papers

Civil service exams are usually identified by number only. You will be assigned a number; you must not put your name on your test papers. Be sure to copy your number correctly. Since more than one exam may be given, copy your exact examination title.

4) Plan your time

Unless you are told that a test is a "speed" or "rate of work" test, speed itself is usually not important. Time enough to answer all the questions will be provided, but this does not mean that you have all day. An overall time limit has been set. Divide the total time (in minutes) by the number of questions to determine the approximate time you have for each question.

5) Do not linger over difficult questions

If you come across a difficult question, mark it with a paper clip (useful to have along) and come back to it when you have been through the booklet. One caution if you do this – be sure to skip a number on your answer sheet as well. Check often to be sure that you have not lost your place and that you are marking in the row numbered the same as the question you are answering.

6) Read the questions

Be sure you know what the question asks! Many capable people are unsuccessful because they failed to *read* the questions correctly.

7) Answer all questions

Unless you have been instructed that a penalty will be deducted for incorrect answers, it is better to guess than to omit a question.

8) Speed tests

It is often better NOT to guess on speed tests. It has been found that on timed tests people are tempted to spend the last few seconds before time is called in marking answers at random – without even reading them – in the hope of picking up a few extra points. To discourage this practice, the instructions may warn you that your score will be "corrected" for guessing. That is, a penalty will be applied. The incorrect answers will be deducted from the correct ones, or some other penalty formula will be used.

9) Review your answers

If you finish before time is called, go back to the questions you guessed or omitted to give them further thought. Review other answers if you have time.

10) Return your test materials

If you are ready to leave before others have finished or time is called, take ALL your materials to the monitor and leave quietly. Never take any test material with you. The monitor can discover whose papers are not complete, and taking a test booklet may be grounds for disqualification.

VIII. EXAMINATION TECHNIQUES

1) Read the general instructions carefully. These are usually printed on the first page of the exam booklet. As a rule, these instructions refer to the timing of the examination; the fact that you should not start work until the signal and must stop work at a signal, etc. If there are any *special* instructions, such as a choice of questions to be answered, make sure that you note this instruction carefully.

2) When you are ready to start work on the examination, that is as soon as the signal has been given, read the instructions to each question booklet, underline any key words or phrases, such as *least, best, outline, describe* and the like. In this way you will tend to answer as requested rather than discover on reviewing your paper that you *listed without describing*, that you selected the *worst* choice rather than the *best* choice, etc.

3) If the examination is of the objective or multiple-choice type – that is, each question will also give a series of possible answers: A, B, C or D, and you are called upon to select the best answer and write the letter next to that answer on your answer paper – it is advisable to start answering each question in turn. There may be anywhere from 50 to 100 such questions in the three or four hours allotted and you can see how much time would be taken if you read through all the questions before beginning to answer any. Furthermore, if you come across a question or group of questions which you know would be difficult to answer, it would undoubtedly affect your handling of all the other questions.

4) If the examination is of the essay type and contains but a few questions, it is a moot point as to whether you should read all the questions before starting to answer any one. Of course, if you are given a choice – say five out of seven and the like – then it is essential to read all the questions so you can eliminate the two that are most difficult. If, however, you are asked to answer all the questions, there may be danger in trying to answer the easiest one first because you may find that you will spend too much time on it. The best technique is to answer the first question, then proceed to the second, etc.

5) Time your answers. Before the exam begins, write down the time it started, then add the time allowed for the examination and write down the time it must be completed, then divide the time available somewhat as follows:
   - If 3-1/2 hours are allowed, that would be 210 minutes. If you have 80 objective-type questions, that would be an average of 2-1/2 minutes per question. Allow yourself no more than 2 minutes per question, or a total of 160 minutes, which will permit about 50 minutes to review.
   - If for the time allotment of 210 minutes there are 7 essay questions to answer, that would average about 30 minutes a question. Give yourself only 25 minutes per question so that you have about 35 minutes to review.

6) The most important instruction is to *read each question* and make sure you know what is wanted. The second most important instruction is to *time yourself properly* so that you answer every question. The third most important instruction is to *answer every question*. Guess if you have to but include something for each question. Remember that you will receive no credit for a blank and will probably receive some credit if you write something in answer to an essay question. If you guess a letter – say "B" for a multiple-choice question – you may have guessed right. If you leave a blank as an answer to a multiple-choice question, the examiners may respect your feelings but it will not add a point to your score. Some exams may penalize you for wrong answers, so in such cases *only*, you may not want to guess unless you have some basis for your answer.

7) Suggestions
   a. Objective-type questions
      1. Examine the question booklet for proper sequence of pages and questions
      2. Read all instructions carefully
      3. Skip any question which seems too difficult; return to it after all other questions have been answered
      4. Apportion your time properly; do not spend too much time on any single question or group of questions

5. Note and underline key words – *all, most, fewest, least, best, worst, same, opposite,* etc.
6. Pay particular attention to negatives
7. Note unusual option, e.g., unduly long, short, complex, different or similar in content to the body of the question
8. Observe the use of "hedging" words – *probably, may, most likely,* etc.
9. Make sure that your answer is put next to the same number as the question
10. Do not second-guess unless you have good reason to believe the second answer is definitely more correct
11. Cross out original answer if you decide another answer is more accurate; do not erase until you are ready to hand your paper in
12. Answer all questions; guess unless instructed otherwise
13. Leave time for review

b. Essay questions
 1. Read each question carefully
 2. Determine exactly what is wanted. Underline key words or phrases.
 3. Decide on outline or paragraph answer
 4. Include many different points and elements unless asked to develop any one or two points or elements
 5. Show impartiality by giving pros and cons unless directed to select one side only
 6. Make and write down any assumptions you find necessary to answer the questions
 7. Watch your English, grammar, punctuation and choice of words
 8. Time your answers; don't crowd material

8) Answering the essay question

Most essay questions can be answered by framing the specific response around several key words or ideas. Here are a few such key words or ideas:

M's: manpower, materials, methods, money, management
P's: purpose, program, policy, plan, procedure, practice, problems, pitfalls, personnel, public relations

a. Six basic steps in handling problems:
 1. Preliminary plan and background development
 2. Collect information, data and facts
 3. Analyze and interpret information, data and facts
 4. Analyze and develop solutions as well as make recommendations
 5. Prepare report and sell recommendations
 6. Install recommendations and follow up effectiveness

b. Pitfalls to avoid
 1. *Taking things for granted* – A statement of the situation does not necessarily imply that each of the elements is necessarily true; for example, a complaint may be invalid and biased so that all that can be taken for granted is that a complaint has been registered

2. *Considering only one side of a situation* – Wherever possible, indicate several alternatives and then point out the reasons you selected the best one
3. *Failing to indicate follow up* – Whenever your answer indicates action on your part, make certain that you will take proper follow-up action to see how successful your recommendations, procedures or actions turn out to be
4. *Taking too long in answering any single question* – Remember to time your answers properly

IX. AFTER THE TEST

Scoring procedures differ in detail among civil service jurisdictions although the general principles are the same. Whether the papers are hand-scored or graded by machine we have described, they are nearly always graded by number. That is, the person who marks the paper knows only the number – never the name – of the applicant. Not until all the papers have been graded will they be matched with names. If other tests, such as training and experience or oral interview ratings have been given, scores will be combined. Different parts of the examination usually have different weights. For example, the written test might count 60 percent of the final grade, and a rating of training and experience 40 percent. In many jurisdictions, veterans will have a certain number of points added to their grades.

After the final grade has been determined, the names are placed in grade order and an eligible list is established. There are various methods for resolving ties between those who get the same final grade – probably the most common is to place first the name of the person whose application was received first. Job offers are made from the eligible list in the order the names appear on it. You will be notified of your grade and your rank as soon as all these computations have been made. This will be done as rapidly as possible.

People who are found to meet the requirements in the announcement are called "eligibles." Their names are put on a list of eligible candidates. An eligible's chances of getting a job depend on how high he stands on this list and how fast agencies are filling jobs from the list.

When a job is to be filled from a list of eligibles, the agency asks for the names of people on the list of eligibles for that job. When the civil service commission receives this request, it sends to the agency the names of the three people highest on this list. Or, if the job to be filled has specialized requirements, the office sends the agency the names of the top three persons who meet these requirements from the general list.

The appointing officer makes a choice from among the three people whose names were sent to him. If the selected person accepts the appointment, the names of the others are put back on the list to be considered for future openings.

That is the rule in hiring from all kinds of eligible lists, whether they are for typist, carpenter, chemist, or something else. For every vacancy, the appointing officer has his choice of any one of the top three eligibles on the list. This explains why the person whose name is on top of the list sometimes does not get an appointment when some of the persons lower on the list do. If the appointing officer chooses the second or third eligible, the No. 1 eligible does not get a job at once, but stays on the list until he is appointed or the list is terminated.

X. HOW TO PASS THE INTERVIEW TEST

The examination for which you applied requires an oral interview test. You have already taken the written test and you are now being called for the interview test – the final part of the formal examination.

You may think that it is not possible to prepare for an interview test and that there are no procedures to follow during an interview. Our purpose is to point out some things you can do in advance that will help you and some good rules to follow and pitfalls to avoid while you are being interviewed.

What is an interview supposed to test?

The written examination is designed to test the technical knowledge and competence of the candidate; the oral is designed to evaluate intangible qualities, not readily measured otherwise, and to establish a list showing the relative fitness of each candidate – as measured against his competitors – for the position sought. Scoring is not on the basis of "right" and "wrong," but on a sliding scale of values ranging from "not passable" to "outstanding." As a matter of fact, it is possible to achieve a relatively low score without a single "incorrect" answer because of evident weakness in the qualities being measured.

Occasionally, an examination may consist entirely of an oral test – either an individual or a group oral. In such cases, information is sought concerning the technical knowledges and abilities of the candidate, since there has been no written examination for this purpose. More commonly, however, an oral test is used to supplement a written examination.

Who conducts interviews?

The composition of oral boards varies among different jurisdictions. In nearly all, a representative of the personnel department serves as chairman. One of the members of the board may be a representative of the department in which the candidate would work. In some cases, "outside experts" are used, and, frequently, a businessman or some other representative of the general public is asked to serve. Labor and management or other special groups may be represented. The aim is to secure the services of experts in the appropriate field.

However the board is composed, it is a good idea (and not at all improper or unethical) to ascertain in advance of the interview who the members are and what groups they represent. When you are introduced to them, you will have some idea of their backgrounds and interests, and at least you will not stutter and stammer over their names.

What should be done before the interview?

While knowledge about the board members is useful and takes some of the surprise element out of the interview, there is other preparation which is more substantive. It *is* possible to prepare for an oral interview – in several ways:

1) Keep a copy of your application and review it carefully before the interview

This may be the only document before the oral board, and the starting point of the interview. Know what education and experience you have listed there, and the sequence and dates of all of it. Sometimes the board will ask you to review the highlights of your experience for them; you should not have to hem and haw doing it.

2) Study the class specification and the examination announcement

Usually, the oral board has one or both of these to guide them. The qualities, characteristics or knowledges required by the position sought are stated in these documents. They offer valuable clues as to the nature of the oral interview. For example, if the job involves supervisory responsibilities, the announcement will usually indicate that knowledge of modern supervisory methods and the qualifications of the candidate as a supervisor will be tested. If so, you can expect such questions, frequently in the form of a hypothetical situation which you are expected to solve. NEVER go into an oral without knowledge of the duties and responsibilities of the job you seek.

3) Think through each qualification required

Try to visualize the kind of questions you would ask if you were a board member. How well could you answer them? Try especially to appraise your own knowledge and background in each area, *measured against the job sought*, and identify any areas in which you are weak. Be critical and realistic – do not flatter yourself.

4) Do some general reading in areas in which you feel you may be weak

For example, if the job involves supervision and your past experience has NOT, some general reading in supervisory methods and practices, particularly in the field of human relations, might be useful. Do NOT study agency procedures or detailed manuals. The oral board will be testing your understanding and capacity, not your memory.

5) Get a good night's sleep and watch your general health and mental attitude

You will want a clear head at the interview. Take care of a cold or any other minor ailment, and of course, no hangovers.

What should be done on the day of the interview?

Now comes the day of the interview itself. Give yourself plenty of time to get there. Plan to arrive somewhat ahead of the scheduled time, particularly if your appointment is in the fore part of the day. If a previous candidate fails to appear, the board might be ready for you a bit early. By early afternoon an oral board is almost invariably behind schedule if there are many candidates, and you may have to wait. Take along a book or magazine to read, or your application to review, but leave any extraneous material in the waiting room when you go in for your interview. In any event, relax and compose yourself.

The matter of dress is important. The board is forming impressions about you – from your experience, your manners, your attitude, and your appearance. Give your personal appearance careful attention. Dress your best, but not your flashiest. Choose conservative, appropriate clothing, and be sure it is immaculate. This is a business interview, and your appearance should indicate that you regard it as such. Besides, being well groomed and properly dressed will help boost your confidence.

Sooner or later, someone will call your name and escort you into the interview room. *This is it.* From here on you are on your own. It is too late for any more preparation. But remember, you asked for this opportunity to prove your fitness, and you are here because your request was granted.

What happens when you go in?

The usual sequence of events will be as follows: The clerk (who is often the board stenographer) will introduce you to the chairman of the oral board, who will introduce you to the other members of the board. Acknowledge the introductions before you sit down. Do not be surprised if you find a microphone facing you or a stenotypist sitting by. Oral interviews are usually recorded in the event of an appeal or other review.

Usually the chairman of the board will open the interview by reviewing the highlights of your education and work experience from your application – primarily for the benefit of the other members of the board, as well as to get the material into the record. Do not interrupt or comment unless there is an error or significant misinterpretation; if that is the case, do not hesitate. But do not quibble about insignificant matters. Also, he will usually ask you some question about your education, experience or your present job – partly to get you to start talking and to establish the interviewing "rapport." He may start the actual questioning, or turn it over to one of the other members. Frequently, each member undertakes the questioning on a particular area, one in which he is perhaps most competent, so you can expect each member to participate in the examination. Because time is limited, you may also expect some rather abrupt switches in the direction the questioning takes, so do not be upset by it. Normally, a board member will not pursue a single line of questioning unless he discovers a particular strength or weakness.

After each member has participated, the chairman will usually ask whether any member has any further questions, then will ask you if you have anything you wish to add. Unless you are expecting this question, it may floor you. Worse, it may start you off on an extended, extemporaneous speech. The board is not usually seeking more information. The question is principally to offer you a last opportunity to present further qualifications or to indicate that you have nothing to add. So, if you feel that a significant qualification or characteristic has been overlooked, it is proper to point it out in a sentence or so. Do not compliment the board on the thoroughness of their examination – they have been sketchy, and you know it. If you wish, merely say, "No thank you, I have nothing further to add." This is a point where you can "talk yourself out" of a good impression or fail to present an important bit of information. Remember, *you close the interview yourself*.

The chairman will then say, "That is all, Mr. _____, thank you." Do not be startled; the interview is over, and quicker than you think. Thank him, gather your belongings and take your leave. Save your sigh of relief for the other side of the door.

How to put your best foot forward

Throughout this entire process, you may feel that the board individually and collectively is trying to pierce your defenses, seek out your hidden weaknesses and embarrass and confuse you. Actually, this is not true. They are obliged to make an appraisal of your qualifications for the job you are seeking, and they want to see you in your best light. Remember, they must interview all candidates and a non-cooperative candidate may become a failure in spite of their best efforts to bring out his qualifications. Here are 15 suggestions that will help you:

1) Be natural – Keep your attitude confident, not cocky

If you are not confident that you can do the job, do not expect the board to be. Do not apologize for your weaknesses, try to bring out your strong points. The board is interested in a positive, not negative, presentation. Cockiness will antagonize any board member and make him wonder if you are covering up a weakness by a false show of strength.

2) Get comfortable, but don't lounge or sprawl

Sit erectly but not stiffly. A careless posture may lead the board to conclude that you are careless in other things, or at least that you are not impressed by the importance of the occasion. Either conclusion is natural, even if incorrect. Do not fuss with your clothing, a pencil or an ashtray. Your hands may occasionally be useful to emphasize a point; do not let them become a point of distraction.

3) Do not wisecrack or make small talk

This is a serious situation, and your attitude should show that you consider it as such. Further, the time of the board is limited – they do not want to waste it, and neither should you.

4) Do not exaggerate your experience or abilities

In the first place, from information in the application or other interviews and sources, the board may know more about you than you think. Secondly, you probably will not get away with it. An experienced board is rather adept at spotting such a situation, so do not take the chance.

5) If you know a board member, do not make a point of it, yet do not hide it

Certainly you are not fooling him, and probably not the other members of the board. Do not try to take advantage of your acquaintanceship – it will probably do you little good.

6) Do not dominate the interview

Let the board do that. They will give you the clues – do not assume that you have to do all the talking. Realize that the board has a number of questions to ask you, and do not try to take up all the interview time by showing off your extensive knowledge of the answer to the first one.

7) Be attentive

You only have 20 minutes or so, and you should keep your attention at its sharpest throughout. When a member is addressing a problem or question to you, give him your undivided attention. Address your reply principally to him, but do not exclude the other board members.

8) Do not interrupt

A board member may be stating a problem for you to analyze. He will ask you a question when the time comes. Let him state the problem, and wait for the question.

9) Make sure you understand the question

Do not try to answer until you are sure what the question is. If it is not clear, restate it in your own words or ask the board member to clarify it for you. However, do not haggle about minor elements.

10) Reply promptly but not hastily

A common entry on oral board rating sheets is "candidate responded readily," or "candidate hesitated in replies." Respond as promptly and quickly as you can, but do not jump to a hasty, ill-considered answer.

11) Do not be peremptory in your answers

A brief answer is proper – but do not fire your answer back. That is a losing game from your point of view. The board member can probably ask questions much faster than you can answer them.

12) Do not try to create the answer you think the board member wants

He is interested in what kind of mind you have and how it works – not in playing games. Furthermore, he can usually spot this practice and will actually grade you down on it.

13) Do not switch sides in your reply merely to agree with a board member

Frequently, a member will take a contrary position merely to draw you out and to see if you are willing and able to defend your point of view. Do not start a debate, yet do not surrender a good position. If a position is worth taking, it is worth defending.

14) Do not be afraid to admit an error in judgment if you are shown to be wrong
The board knows that you are forced to reply without any opportunity for careful consideration. Your answer may be demonstrably wrong. If so, admit it and get on with the interview.

15) Do not dwell at length on your present job
The opening question may relate to your present assignment. Answer the question but do not go into an extended discussion. You are being examined for a *new* job, not your present one. As a matter of fact, try to phrase ALL your answers in terms of the job for which you are being examined.

Basis of Rating

Probably you will forget most of these "do's" and "don'ts" when you walk into the oral interview room. Even remembering them all will not ensure you a passing grade. Perhaps you did not have the qualifications in the first place. But remembering them will help you to put your best foot forward, without treading on the toes of the board members.

Rumor and popular opinion to the contrary notwithstanding, an oral board wants you to make the best appearance possible. They know you are under pressure – but they also want to see how you respond to it as a guide to what your reaction would be under the pressures of the job you seek. They will be influenced by the degree of poise you display, the personal traits you show and the manner in which you respond.

ABOUT THIS BOOK

This book contains tests divided into Examination Sections. Go through each test, answering every question in the margin. We have also attached a sample answer sheet at the back of the book that can be removed and used. At the end of each test look at the answer key and check your answers. On the ones you got wrong, look at the right answer choice and learn. Do not fill in the answers first. Do not memorize the questions and answers, but understand the answer and principles involved. On your test, the questions will likely be different from the samples. Questions are changed and new ones added. If you understand these past questions you should have success with any changes that arise. Tests may consist of several types of questions. We have additional books on each subject should more study be advisable or necessary for you. Finally, the more you study, the better prepared you will be. This book is intended to be the last thing you study before you walk into the examination room. Prior study of relevant texts is also recommended. NLC publishes some of these in our Fundamental Series. Knowledge and good sense are important factors in passing your exam. Good luck also helps. So now study this Passbook, absorb the material contained within and take that knowledge into the examination. Then do your best to pass that exam.

EXAMINATION SECTION

EXAMINATION SECTION
TEST 1

DIRECTIONS: Each question or incomplete statement is followed by several suggested answers or completions. Select the one that BEST answers the question or completes the statement. *PRINT THE LETTER OF THE CORRECT ANSWER IN THE SPACE AT THE RIGHT.*

Questions 1-23.

DIRECTIONS: Find the word which means the same or most nearly the same as the italicized word.

1. *good*
   A. late   B. nice   C. to   D. green   E. much

2. *lady*
   A. like   B. woman   C. gracious   D. girl   E. man

3. *bring*
   a. were   B. use   C. carry   D. put   E. sleep

4. *speak*
   A. silent   B. shout   C. whisper   D. talk   E. gossip

5. *quick*
   A. run   B. slow   C. sand   D. men   E. fast

6. *scorch*
   A. scent   B. cook   C. run   D. burn   E. flaunt

7. *space*
   A. school   B. noon   C. room   D. captain   E. board

8. *confess*
   A. agree   B. admit   C. mend   D. deny   E. mingle

9. *donate*
   A. donor   B. giver   C. give   D. doughnut   E. gift

10. *strength*
    A. heavy   B. importance   C. long
    D. immense   E. power

11. *escort*
    A. follow   B. court   C. defend
    D. accompany   E. accomplish

1.____
2.____
3.____
4.____
5.____
6.____
7.____
8.____
9.____
10.____
11.____

12. *blunt*
    A. drowsy B. bluff C. doubtful D. ugly E. dull 12._____

13. *regulation*
    A. police B. obey C. proper D. rule E. regular 13._____

14. *bouillon*
    A. cracker B. animal C. soup D. play E. metal 14._____

15. *concur*
    A. race B. mongrel C. pounce D. agree E. ramble 15._____

16. *cambric*
    A. tea B. town C. wood D. maggot E. cloth 16._____

17. *limerick*
    A. clown B. novel C. ruling D. verse E. automobile 17._____

18. *average*
    A. level B. count C. evident D. ordinary E. distinct 18._____

19. *reality*
    A. real B. actuality C. safe D. true E. real estate 19._____

20. *perfunctory*
    A. careless B. orderly C. salt D. wit E. officer 20._____

21. *habitat*
    A. home B. dweller C. bodice D. habit E. custom 21._____

22. *obeisance*
    A. fear B. curtsy C. sycophantic
    D. hidden E. obedience 22._____

23. *largess*
    A. enormity B. gift C. size
    D. amiability E. monstrosity 23._____

KEY (CORRECT ANSWERS)

1.	B		11.	D
2.	B		12.	E
3.	C		13.	D
4.	D		14.	C
5.	E		15.	D
6.	D		16.	E
7.	C		17.	D
8.	B		18.	D
9.	C		19.	B
10.	E		20.	A

21. A
22. B
23. B

TEST 2

DIRECTIONS: Each question or incomplete statement is followed by several suggested answers or completions. Select the one that BEST answers the question or completes the statement. *PRINT THE LETTER OF THE CORRECT ANSWER IN THE SPACE AT THE RIGHT.*

Questions 1-22.

DIRECTIONS: In Questions 1 through 22, find the thing that the italicized word is most likely to have.

1. *A bay always has*   1.____
   A. sand   B. water   C. rocks   D. ships   E. a seaport

2. *A square*   2.____
   A. 5 sides   B. 4 sides   C. 5 corners   D. 6 corners   E. 8 corners

3. *A baby*   3.____
   A. mouth   B. bottle   C. carriage   D. sister   E. brother

4. *A boy*   4.____
   A. coat   B. sister   C. birthday   D. brother   E. shoes

5. *A tree*   5.____
   A. leaves   B. squirrels   C. nests   D. roots   E. fruit

6. *A crowd*   6.____
   A. people   B. noise   C. leader   D. speaker   E. excitement

7. *A man*   7.____
   A. clothes   B. head   C. home   D. money   E. legs

8. *A saw*   8.____
   A. carpenter   B. sharpness   C. teeth
   D. bluntness   E. wood

9. *A fountain pen*   9.____
   A. paper   B. ink container   C. ink
   D. gold point   E. pocket clip

10. *A museum*   10.____
    A. collections   B. animals   C. stones
    D. minerals   E. visitors

11. *A lake*   11.____
    A. trees   B. fish   C. sand   D. water   E. boats

2 (#2)

12. *A piano*
    A. music   B. player   C. keys   D. lamp   E. stool

    12.____

13. *A mountain*
    A. snow   B. a summit   C. trees   D. springs   E. lava

    13.____

14. *A cup*
    A. handle   B. coffee   C. tea   D. rim   E. a saucer

    14.____

15. *A bottle*
    A. glass   B. base   C. liquid   D. stopper   E. roundness

    15.____

16. *A banquet*
    A. ice cream   B. music   C. food
    D. speeches   E. flowers

    16.____

17. *A plate*
    A. roundness   B. food   C. dimensions
    D. beauty   E. whiteness

    17.____

18. *A debate*
    A. chairman   B. chairs   C. audience
    D. opponents   E. fighting

    18.____

19. *A wheel*
    A. a center   B. spokes   C. a tire   D. paint   E. steel

    19.____

20. *Water*
    A. germs   B. volume   C. faucets   D. minerals   E. sweetness

    20.____

21. *Money*
    A. roundness   B. gold   C. an owner
    D. denomination   E. U.S.A.

    21.____

22. *A typewriter*
    A. paper   B. typist   C. keys   D. ribbon   E. desk

    22.____

5

KEY (CORRECT ANSWERS)

1.	B	11.	D
2.	B	12.	C
3.	A	13.	B
4.	C	14.	D
5.	D	15.	B
6.	A	16.	C
7.	B	17.	C
8.	C	18.	D
9.	B	19.	A
10.	A	20.	B

21. D
22. C

TEST 3

DIRECTIONS: Each question or incomplete statement is followed by several suggested answers or completions. Select the one that BEST answers the question or completes the statement. *PRINT THE LETTER OF THE CORRECT ANSWER IN THE SPACE AT THE RIGHT.*

Questions 1-23.

DIRECTIONS: In answering Questions 1 through 23, select the number which comes next.

1. 2 3 4 5 6 7
    A. 8   B. 9   C. 11   D. 10   E. 12   1.____

2. 1 1 2 2 3 3
    A. 5   B. 4   C. 3   D. 2   E. 1   2.____

3. 8 7 6 5 4 3
    A. 3   B. 5   C. 2   D. 1   E. 4   3.____

4. 7 0 8 0 9 0
    A. 6   B. 11   C. 12   D. 10   E. 9   4.____

5. 10 15 20 25 30 35
    A. 45   B. 50   C. 36   D. 40   E. 65   5.____

6. 2 4 6 8 10 12
    A. 13   B. 17   C. 15   D. 16   E. 14   6.____

7. 4 6 8 10 12 14
    A. 15   B. 13   C. 16   D. 10   E. 14   7.____

8. ½ 1 1½ 2 2½ 3
    A. 4   B. 3½   C. 4½   D. 3¼   E. 5   8.____

9. 21 19 17 15 13 11
    A. 10   B. 15   C. 21   D. 9   E. 12   9.____

10. 16 32 8 16 4 8
    A. 6   B. 8   C. ½   D. 4   E. 2   10.____

11. 2 5 4 5 6 5
    A. 10   B. 5   C. 8   D. 3   E. 7   11.____

12. 18 21 24 27 30 33
    A. 36   B. 43   C. 39   D. 31   D. 34   12.____

2 (#3)

13. 17 15 13 11 9 7
    A. 8   B. 4   C. 6   D. 9   E. 5   13.____

14. 51 60 71 80 91 100
    A. 121   B. 131   C. 120   D. 111   E. 109   14.____

15. 3 4 6 9 13 18
    A. 17   B. 19   C. 23   D. 24   E. 26   15.____

16. 64 32 16 8 4 2
    A. 0   B. 4   C. 1   D. 6   E. 8   16.____

17. 17 15 12 10 7 5
    A. 2   B. 4   C. 6   D. 7   E. 3   17.____

18. 2/3 1 1 1/3 1 2/3 2 2 1/3
    A. 2 2/3   B. 3 2/3   C. 2 1/3   D. 2   E. 3   18.____

19. 4 9 16 25 36 49
    A. 57   B. 64   C. 43   D. 68   E. 70   19.____

20. 8 11 11 14 14 17
    A. 19   B. 17   C. 20   D. 16   E. 18   20.____

21. 3 8 15 24 35 48
    A. 58   B. 55   C. 63   D. 61   E. 71   21.____

22. 32 16 8 4 2 1
    A. 2   B. 4   C. ½   D. 1   E. 0   22.____

23. 10 20 40 50 100 110
    A. 115   B. 120   C. 320   D. 220   E. 90   23.____

KEY (CORRECT ANSWERS)

1.	A	11.	C
2.	B	12.	A
3.	C	13.	E
4.	D	14.	D
5.	D	15.	D
6.	E	16.	C
7.	C	17.	A
8.	B	18.	A
9.	D	19.	B
10.	E	20.	B

21. C
22. C
23. D

TEST 4

DIRECTIONS: Each question or incomplete statement is followed by several suggested answers or completions. Select the one that BEST answers the question or completes the statement. *PRINT THE LETTER OF THE CORRECT ANSWER IN THE SPACE AT THE RIGHT.*

1. An army is required because
    A. the country needs protection
    B. people like soldiers
    C. pacifists must be silenced
    D. it is good for physical training
    E. it employs a great many men

    1.____

2. Life insurance is a benefit to the people because it
    A. helps the poor
    B. helps to protect their future
    C. is the modern-day custom
    D. prevents people from dying too soon
    E. increases business

    2.____

3. A harbor is considered a good one if it
    A. is long and shallow
    B. is in Europe
    C. is sheltered and deep
    D. is built of stone
    E. has many ships

    3.____

4. People pay taxes because they
    A. must support the government
    B. must help the poor
    C. must elect governors
    D. are too rich
    E. like to do so

    4.____

5. Graphite is used for pencils because
    A. it writes clearly and erases easily
    B. lead costs more
    C. it can be erased more easily than ink
    D. it is found in mines
    E. it looks beautiful

    5.____

6. Laws are made because
    A. they are to be obeyed by everyone
    B. modern society needs them
    C. they safeguard our automobiles
    D. the legislature has been elected
    E. all men are dishonest

    6.____

7. "Birds of a feather flock together" means:
    A. All crows fly together in one flock
    B. People of a kind don't mind
    C. People with the same interests associate with each other
    D. We all like to do the same thing
    E. Time and tide wait for no man

    7.____

2 (#4)

8. Most tall trees are tall because 8.____
   A. sunlight falls on them
   B. they belong to a tall species
   C. they grow near orchards
   D. they are neglected
   E. they are evergreens

9. "All that glitters is not gold" means: 9.____
   A. You cannot judge a book by its cover
   B. Gold does not glitter as a diamond
   C. Only little things shine
   D. Some glittering things are silver
   E. The best things are made of gold

10. "Learning is a scepter to some, a bauble to others" means: 10.____
    A. Learn not, and know not
    B. Knowledge is power to him who knows how to use it
    C. Learning makes a good man better and an evil man worse
    D. Learning is the most important thing in life
    E. A little learning is a dangerous thing

11. The reason gold is so valuable is that it 11.____
    A. can be mined only with difficulty
    B. does not tarnish
    C. is relatively a rare metal
    D. shines brighter than other metals
    E. is found in this country

12. It is useful to know how to swim because 12.____
    A. lakes are often very deep
    B. it is a healthful exercise
    C. all animals know how to swim
    D. swimming is faster than walking
    E. one may fall into deep water

13. Furniture is usually made of wood because wood 13.____
    A. can be polished
    B. burns more easily than coal
    C. looks better than steel
    D. is cheap and easily worked
    E. lasts longer than steel

14. "Such a father, such a son" means: 14.____
    A. Such a welcome, such a farewell
    B. Such is the government, such are the people
    C. Such is the morning, such is the evening
    D. Such is the hour, such is the man
    E. Such is a tree, such is the fruit

15. Money was invented because 15.____
    A. people could have more jobs coining it
    B. it increases the wealth of the country
    C. it is not easy to counterfeit
    D. it provides for a standard medium of exchange
    E. it can easily be hidden

16. "Strike when the iron is hot" means:
    A. A danger foreseen is half avoided
    B. Grind with every wind
    C. A burnt child dreads the fire
    D. Cold metal does not bend
    E. Put your shoulder to the wheel

16.____

KEY (CORRECT ANSWERS)

1.	A	11.	C
2.	B	12.	E
3.	C	13.	D
4.	A	14.	E
5.	A	15.	D
6.	B	16.	B
7.	C		
8.	B		
9.	A		
10.	B		

TEST 5

DIRECTIONS: Each question or incomplete statement is followed by several suggested answers or completions. Select the one that BEST answers the question or completes the statement. *PRINT THE LETTER OF THE CORRECT ANSWER IN THE SPACE AT THE RIGHT.*

Questions 1-23.

DIRECTIONS: In each of Questions 1 through 23, there is one word which does not belong with the others. PRINT THE LETTER OF THE CORRECT ANSWER IN THE SPACE AT THE RIGHT.

1. A. crow B. sparrow C. robin D. dog E. swallow 1.____

2. A. forks B. spoons C. knives D. soup E. dishes 2.____

3. A. horses B. tigers C. chickens D. lions E. foxes 3.____

4. A. eyes B. hair C. ears D. nose E. mouth 4.____

5. A. United States B. North America C. Europe 5.____
   D. Asia E. Africa

6. A. inches B. minutes C. yards D. feet D. rods 6.____

7. A. bed B. chair C. window D. stool E. table 7.____

8. A. Lincoln B. Washington C. Roosevelt 8.____
   D. Lafayette E. Wilson

9. A. John B. Mary C. Jones D. Alice E. William 9.____

10. A. mittens B. socks C. shoes D. boots E. stockings 10.____

11. A. houses B. autos C. barns D. garages E. stores 11.____

12. A. sidewalk B. wall C. ceiling 12.____
    D. floor E. roof

13. A. snow B. sunshine C. rain D. hail E. fog 13.____

14. A. circus B. opera C. school D. theater E. movies 14.____

15. A. Columbus B. Penn C. Cabot 15.____
    D. Hudson E. Magellan

16. A. halt B. go C. advance D. progress E. proceed 16.____

13

2 (#5)

17. A. letter B. messenger C. message 17.____
    D. note E. telegram

18. A. duke B. senator C. count D. king E. marquis 18.____

19. A. book B. volume C. magazine 19.____
    D. bookcase E. pamphlet

20. A. second B. week C. day D. month E. moment 20.____

21. A. yards B. degrees C. minutes D. gallons E. rulers 21.____

22. A. shoes B. dishes C. pictures D. fruits E. tires 22.____

23. A. physician B. dentist C. surgeon 23.____
    D. botanist E. nurse

KEY (CORRECT ANSWERS)

1.	D		11.	B
2.	D		12.	A
3.	C		13.	B
4.	B		14.	C
5.	A		15.	B
6.	B		16.	A
7.	C		17.	B
8.	D		18.	B
9.	C		19.	D
10.	A		20.	E

21. E
22. D
23. D

TEST 6

DIRECTIONS: Each question or incomplete statement is followed by several suggested answers or completions. Select the one that BEST answers the question or completes the statement. *PRINT THE LETTER OF THE CORRECT ANSWER IN THE SPACE AT THE RIGHT.*

Questions 1-22.

DIRECTIONS: In each of Questions 1 through 22 one of the lettered words is the *opposite* or nearly the opposite of the italicized word. PRINT THE LETTER OF THE CORRECT ANSWER IN THE SPACE AT THE RIGHT.

1. *yes*
   A. all right   B. not   C. always   D. no   E. O.K.

2. *thick*
   A. friendly   B. wafer   C. paste   D. thin   E. compact

3. *stormy*
   A. inclement   B. weather   C. cyclone
   D. dark   E. fair

4. *asleep*
   A. drowsy   B. lively   C. awake   D. lazy   E. sleepy

5. *sorry*
   A. laughing   B. glad   C. cripple   D. angry   E. pitiful

6. *pretty*
   A. good   B. bad   C. worse   D. crooked   E. ugly

7. *raise*
   A. wheat   B. risen   C. down   D. lower   E. window

8. *hate*
   A. joy   B. good   C. love   D. friend   E. enemy

9. *keen*
   A. steep   B. knife   C. pointed   D. blunt   E. rounded

10. *continue*
    A. proceed   B. restrain   C. apply   D. reverse   E. cease

11. *open*
    A. door   B. shut   C. barred   D. wide   E. key

12. *inclement*
    - A. blank
    - B. stormy
    - C. salubrious
    - D. rainy
    - E. clemency

    12.____

13. *destroy*
    - A. alter
    - B. destruction
    - C. deliver
    - D. restore
    - E. continue

    13.____

14. *hope*
    - A. faith
    - B. despair
    - C. misery
    - D. sorrow
    - E. hate

    14.____

15. *slavery*
    - A. trader
    - B. bondage
    - C. justice
    - D. freedom
    - E. equality

    15.____

16. *accept*
    - A. admit
    - B. receive
    - C. reject
    - D. spend
    - E. deny

    16.____

17. *masculine*
    - A. woman
    - B. man
    - C. feminine
    - D. female
    - E. master

    17.____

18. *mild*
    - A. strength
    - B. severe
    - C. weather
    - D. difficult
    - E. bitter

    18.____

19. *lazy*
    - A. slow
    - B. idle
    - C. plodding
    - D. quick
    - E. industrious

    19.____

20. *crazy*
    - A. insane
    - B. clever
    - C. stupid
    - D. sane
    - E. brilliant

    20.____

21. *infinite*
    - A. infidel
    - B. limited
    - C. small
    - D. inform
    - E. large

    21.____

22. *cheerless*
    - A. attitude
    - B. courageous
    - C. joyful
    - D. disconsolate
    - E. merciful

    22.____

KEY (CORRECT ANSWERS)

1. D
2. D
3. E
4. C
5. B

6. E
7. D
8. C
9. D
10. E

11. B
12. C
13. D
14. B
15. D

16. C
17. C
18. B
19. E
20. D

21. B
22. C

TEST 7

DIRECTIONS: Each question or incomplete statement is followed by several suggested answers or completions. Select the one that BEST answers the question or completes the statement. *PRINT THE LETTER OF THE CORRECT ANSWER IN THE SPACE AT THE RIGHT.*

Questions 1-23.

DIRECTIONS: In Questions 1 through 23, the third word is related to one of the lettered words as the first word is related to the second. PRINT THE LETTER OF THE CORRECT LETTERED WORK IN THE SPACE AT THE RIGHT.

1. theater – people :: hive -
   A. thrive   B. sting   C. thick   D. ants   E. bees   1.____

2. hand – arm :: foot -
   A. toe   B. finger   C. wrist   D. leg   E. elbow   2.____

3. straw – hat :: leather -
   A. feather   B. cool   C. shoe   D. soft   E. hard   3.____

4. foot – man :: hoof -
   A. leather   B. cow   C. shoe   D. leg   E. woman   4.____

5. go – come :: sell -
   A. leave   B. buy   C. money   D. paper   E. give   5.____

6. hour – minute :: minute -
   A. second   B. man   C. week   D. short   E. sixty   6.____

7. left – right :: west -
   A. south   B. direction   C. east   D. north   E. compass   7.____

8. peeling – banana :: shell -
   A. skin   B. orange   C. juice   D. egg   E. ripe   8.____

9. granary – wheat :: library -
   A. desk   B. books   C. paper   D. librarian   E. building   9.____

10. table – wood :: stove -
    A. iron   B. bottle   C. paper   D. cork   E. burns   10.____

11. man – boy :: sheep -
    A. wool   B. goat   C. lamb   D. shepherd   E. dog   11.____

12. officer – private :: command -
    A. army   B. general   C. regiment   D. weapon   E. obey   12.____

2 (#7)

13. moon – earth :: earth -
    A. sun   B. light   C. Mars   D. star   E. comet   13.____

14. reward – hero :: punish -
    A. God   B. traitor   C. everlasting   14.____
    D. pain   E. death

15. sand – glass :: clay -
    A. stone   B. bricks   C. hay   D. dirt   E. house   15.____

16. thou – thee :: we -
    A. they   B. I   C. us   D. you   E. them   16.____

17. engineer – engine :: driver -
    A. harness   B. passenger   C. man   17.____
    D. railroad   E. horse

18. city – mayor :: army -
    A. soldier   B. navy   C. private   D. arms   E. general   18.____

19. peace – happiness :: war -
    A. fright   B. battle   C. Europe   D. sorrow   E. joy   19.____

20. known – unknown :: present -
    A. past   B. expensive   C. Christmas   20.____
    D. future   E. famous

21. abundant – scarce :: cheap -
    A. buy   B. bargain   C. costly   D. nasty   E. expense   21.____

22. float – sink :: cork -
    A. float   B. light   C. lead   D. heavy   E. water   22.____

23. land – peninsula :: ocean -
    A. river   B. gulf   C. lake   D. cape   E. water   23.____

KEY (CORRECT ANSWERS)

1. E
2. D
3. C
4. B
5. B

6. A
7. C
8. D
9. B
10. A

11. C
12. E
13. A
14. B
15. B

16. C
17. E
18. E
19. D
20. D

21. C
22. C
23. B

———

TEST 8

DIRECTIONS: Each question or incomplete statement is followed by several suggested answers or completions. Select the one that BEST answers the question or completes the statement. *PRINT THE LETTER OF THE CORRECT ANSWER IN THE SPACE AT THE RIGHT.*

1. What do you pay in all if you buy a pencil for 5 cents, a pad for 6 cents, and a ruler for 4 cents?
   A. $.34   B. $.07   C. $.05   D. $.54   E. $.15
   1._____

2. Miss Smith's class learns 3 words a day. How many words does the class learn in 9 days?
   A. 6   B. 3   C. 12   D. 27   E. 15
   2._____

3. You buy something for 55 cents and you give the storekeeper $1.00. What change should you receive?
   A. $.55   B. $.25   C. $.45   D. $1.45   E. $.75
   3._____

4. You buy two 2-cent stamps and pay for them with a dime. How much change should you receive?
   A. $.04   B. $.20   C. $.05   D. $.14   E. $.06
   4._____

5. There are 35 children in our class; 14 of them are boys. How many girls are there in the class?
   A. 49   B. 35   C. 17   D. 25   E. 21
   5._____

6. How many Christmas seals are there in a sheet 8 seals wide and 10 seals long?
   A. 18   B. 180   C. 2   D. 80   E. 20
   6._____

7. Mary can buy 3 oranges for 10 cents. How many can she buy for 30 cents?
   A. 20   B. 13   C. 9   D. 3   E. 10
   7._____

8. If John and James have 24 cents to divide equally, how much will each get?
   A. 16   B. 10   C. 14   D. 12   E. 18
   8._____

9. A football team took 14 players on a trip. The trip cost the team $56. How much was that for each player?
   A. $42   B. $70   C. $784   D. $24   E. $4
   9._____

10. Jack walks at the rate of 2 miles an hour. Henry starts with him and runs in the same direction at the rate of 3 miles an hour. How many miles apart will they be in 3½ hours?
    A. 5   B. 1   C. 17½   D. 3½   E. 7
    10._____

11. Mr. Jones buys one dozen brushes at 14 cents each. Mr. Smith buys 12 brushes for $1.50. How much more did Mr. Jones pay than Mr. Smith?
   A. $1.36   B. 12½ cents   C. $.18
   D. $.02   E. $1.64

12. If an airplane travels at 150 miles an hour, how many hours will it take to travel to an airport 1,050 miles away?
   A. 7   B. 1,200   C. 900   D. 10   E. 9

13. A contractor completed 2/3 of a job in 14 days. How many more days should it take him to finish the job?
   A. 14   B. 7   C. 21   D. 28   E. 35

14. A real estate dealer made a gain of $8,000 on the sale of a farm. His gain was 20 percent of the cost. Find the cost of the farm.
   A. $40,000   B. $1,600   C. $160,000   D. $4,000   E. $2,000

15. What is the cost per coat if it costs $43.00 for material and $65.00 for labor for 4 coats?
   A. $108   B. $27   C. $22   D. $266   E. $172

16. What number multiplied by 4 and then divided by ¼ equals 16?
   A. 264   B. 64   C. 16   D. 1   E. 4

KEY (CORRECT ANSWERS)

1.	E	11.	C
2.	D	12.	A
3.	C	13.	B
4.	E	14.	A
5.	E	15.	B
6.	D	16.	D
7.	C		
8.	D		
9.	E		
10.	D		

EXAMINATION SECTION
TEST 1

DIRECTIONS: Each question or incomplete statement is followed by several suggested answers or completions. Select the one that BEST answers the question or completes the statement. *PRINT THE CORRECT ANSWER IN THE SPACE AT THE RIGHT.*

1. Add: 1 1/2
   4 3/4
   9 3/8
   3 7/8

   1.____

2. Subtract: 367 3/8
   149 7/8

   2.____

3. Divide: 15.6)‾2496‾

   3.____

4. Multiply: .0035
   .56

   4.____

5. A, B, and C together can dig a ditch in 12 days. B can dig the same ditch alone in 36 days.
   How long will it take A and C to dig the ditch?

   5.____

6. This is the AYTEENTH day of the month.
   The word in capitals is misspelled. Write it correctly at the right.

   6.____

7. Which one of the following applies to both CITY DIRECTORY and TELEPHONE DIRECTORY but not to DICTIONARY?

   A. Free distribution
   B. Gives information
   C. Alphabetic listing
   D. Gives addresses
   E. Necessary business equipment

   7.____

8. Which is the Executive branch of our government?

   A. Congress   B. Supreme Court
   C. President and Cabinet D. President and Senate
   E. Secretary of State

   8.____

9. NINE is to BASEBALL as ELEVEN is to

   A. dice   B. polo   C. sports
   D. hockey   E. football

   9.____

10. OUNCE is to POUND as QUART is to

    A. liquids   B. bottle   C. peck
    D. measurement   E. milk

    10.____

11. DISC is to SPHERE as SQUARE is to

    A. flat   B. tool   C. circle   D. cube   E. box

    11.____

23

12. PRODUCT is to TRADEMARK as COUNTRY is to   12._____

    A. map   B. governed   C. flag
    D. boundary   E. political unit

13. An invitation requires an AKNAHLEJMENT.   13._____
    The word in capitals is misspelled. Write it correctly at the right.

14. The actress wanted to KANSEL her contract.   14._____
    The word in capitals is misspelled. Write it correctly at the right.

15. Local and long distance telephone service has been an important factor in the laying of a   15._____
    firm foundation for the modern American commercial structure. Upon its direct and per-
    sonal communication depend many millions of the human contacts which must be made
    every day if the nation's business is to be done. Nowhere so widely as in America has
    the telephone been accepted as one of the essential tools of trade. Nowhere else is busi-
    ness transacted more swiftly and more surely. Nowhere else have been laid more
    securely the cornerstones of close cooperation and mutual understanding upon which
    sound business must be built.
    Judging from the above paragraph, which one of the following statements is TRUE?

    A. The telephone is not nearly so widely used in America as elsewhere.
    B. Business deals could not be transacted without telephone service.
    C. The modern American commercial structure has a firmer foundation because of
       the telephone service.
    D. Long distance telephone service is not an important factor in conducting a busi-
       ness.
    E. Foreign nations do not use long distance calls for business.

16. Judging entirely from the above paragraph, it is TRUE that sound business must be built   16._____
    upon

    A. a wide use of the telephone
    B. direct and personal communication
    C. swift and sure methods of doing business
    D. making millions of human contacts
    E. mutual understanding and close cooperation

17. Manufacturers BLEND coffee.   17._____
    In the above sentence, the word BLEND means

    A. drink   B. mix   C. brand
    D. ship   E. imitate

18. He BESTOWS favors.   18._____
    In the above sentence, the word BESTOWS means

    A. receives   B. collects   C. despises
    D. confers   E. refuses

19. ARSON is   19._____

    A. theft   B. murder   C. incendiarism
    D. fraud   E. suicide

20. APATHETIC is 20._____

    A. courteous   B. attentive   C. distracted
    D. unresponsive   E. sympathetic

21. If Jim had a savings bank in which he put 1¢ Monday, three times as much Tuesday as Monday, three times as much Wednesday as Tuesday, etc., until he had a total of $1.21 in the savings bank, how many days did it take to save this amount? 21._____

22. Jack's share of an estate is $6,000, which is 1/5 more than George's share. What is the value of the whole estate? 22._____

23. I sold a dog for $63 at a loss of $12\frac{1}{2}\%$. 23._____

If this dog had been sold for $81 instead, what would the percent of gain have been?

24. What is 1/3 of 10 added to 1/2 of 1/3 of 10? 24._____

25. Which one of the following can be applied to AUDIENCE and SPECTATORS but not to ACTORS? 25._____

    A. Dramatize   B. Rehearsals
    C. Paying attention   D. Not taking part
    E. Attendance

KEY (CORRECT ANSWERS)

1. $19\frac{1}{2}$
2. $217\frac{1}{2}$
3. .016
4. .00196
5. 18
6. eighteenth
7. D
8. C
9. E
10. C
11. D
12. C
13. acknowledgement
14. cancel
15. C
16. E
17. B
18. D
19. C
20. D
21. E
22. $11,000
23. $12\frac{1}{2}\%$
24. E
25. D

TEST 2

DIRECTIONS: Each question or incomplete statement is followed by several suggested answers or completions. Select the one that BEST answers the question or completes the statement. *PRINT THE CORRECT ANSWER IN THE SPACE AT THE RIGHT.*

1. They were well EEKWIPT for the trip.
   The word in capitals is misspelled. Write it correctly at the right.
   1.____

2. There was a NOTISUBUL increase in attendance.
   The word in capitals is misspelled. Write it correctly at the right.
   2.____

3. *When the government caused the great Northwest to be surveyed, it divided the land into squares, each having, as nearly as possible, six miles on a side. These divisions are called townships. A row of townships along a north and south line is called a range. The township is thus seen to be a geographical unit, while a town, which is a political unit, may include one or more townships or less than a township. The town government is almost a democracy, for all the voters may meet once a year and elect their officers and vote money for necessary things for which the state law permits public money to be used.*
   According to the above paragraph, a town
   3.____

   A. must be on a range line
   B. and a township are one and the same thing
   C. should be as nearly square as possible
   D. must include one or more townships
   E. is a political rather than a geographical unit

4. According to the above paragraph,
   4.____

   A. the democratic party always rules in townships
   B. people in towns meet only once each year
   C. towns have a nearly democratic form of government
   D. voters in towns may appropriate money for necessary things only by special permission of the state legislature
   E. town officers vote money only for necessary things

5. ADULT is to CHILD as GOOSE is to
   5.____

   A. younger   B. poultry   C. gander
   D. feathers   E. gosling

6. EAST is to WEST as CONSERVATIVE is to
   6.____

   A. legal   B. travel   C. liberal
   D. politics   E. congress

7. DEER is to WOODS as WHALE is to
   7.____

   A. fish   B. mammal   C. bones   D. huge   E. ocean

8. Which one of the following applies to both POSTMASTER and POST OFFICE DEPARTMENT but not to U.S. TREASURY? 8.____

   A. Municipal
   B. Public building
   C. Authorized to issue postal money orders
   D. Depository for federal funds
   E. Appointed

9. The enemy KAPITYOOLAYTED. 9.____
   The word in capitals is misspelled. Write it correctly at the right.

10. A true VALYOOAYSHUN of property is made. 10.____
    The word in capitals is misspelled. Write it correctly at the right.

11. He explained the PRINSIPULS of his system. 11.____
    The word in capitals is misspelled. Write it correctly at the right.

12. *In 1748, George Washington, while surveying beyond the Blue Ridge, first faced real frontier life and conditions. This was one of the many experiences which taught him the true meaning of isolation and made him an ardent advocate of good highways and adequate communication facilities.* 12.____
    He saw that these facilities would form strong links in the chain of federal union. To him, in large measure, Americans of his day owed their recognition of the value f effective means of keeping the widely separated sections of the country in touch with each other. While Washington was beginning to see at first hand the need for better communication facilities, Franklin was performing, in Philadelphia, a series of electrical experiments that indirectly played an important part in meeting this need. The spark that crossed the Schuylkill foreshadowed the far-flung systems of electrical communication now serving the United States.
    The above paragraph clearly states that

    A. Washington installed the first line for electrical communication between the settlements
    B. Franklin invented the telephone
    C. Franklin was the first man to use electrical communication
    D. good communication facilities between settlements would strengthen the federal union
    E. in Washington's time, electrical communication was the only means of keeping the widely separated sections of the country in touch with each other

13. Audiences hear; spectators 13.____

    A. crowd   B. surge   C. see
    D. are curious   E. run

14. A newsdealer sold 18 magazines for the cost of 24. What is his percent of profit? 14.____

15. *A handsome woman is always right.*
    The above quotation means MOST NEARLY

    A. guilt is always timid
    B. he is armed without that is innocent within
    C. a pretty woman wins the lawsuit
    D. appearances are deceiving
    E. first impressions are lasting impressions

16. A freight train left Atlanta at 8:15 A.M. traveling at the rate of 22 miles per hour. A mail train left Atlanta at 9:45 A.M., passing the freight train at 11:15 A.M. What is the speed per hour of the mail train?

17. To ACCUMULATE is to

    A. scatter   B. amass   C. dissipate
    D. exploit   E. hide

18. An AFFECTIONATE person is one who is

    A. fond   B. harsh   C. kind
    D. pleasant   E. unselfish

19. *Boldly ventured is half won.*
    The above quotation means MOST NEARLY

    A. courage should have eyes as well as ears
    B. fortune gives her hand to the bold man
    C. a bold attempt is half success
    D. be not too bold
    E. looking before leaping is saving from falling

20. To COMPENSATE is to

    A. require   B. reward   C. oblige
    D. abridge   E. understand

21. To CORROBORATE is to

    A. approve   B. confirm   C. contest
    D. refute   E. agree

22. YES is to AFFIRMATIVE as NO is to

    A. knowledge   B. reason   C. negative
    D. think   E. positive

23. A wooden box four inches high and three inches long contains seventy-two cubic inches. How many inches wide is the box?

24. A man sold his house for $8,000, thereby gaining $3,000. What percent did he gain on his investment?

25. The younger male relative of an uncle is a NEFYOO.
    The word in capitals is misspelled. Write it correctly at the right.

KEY (CORRECT ANSWERS)

1. equipped
2. noticeable
3. E
4. C
5. E

6. C
7. E
8. C
9. capitulated
10. valuation

11. principles
12. D
13. C
14. 33 1/3%
15. C

16. 44
17. B
18. A
19. C
20. B

21. B
22. C
23. 6 inches
24. 60%
25. nephew

TEST 3

DIRECTIONS: Each question or incomplete statement is followed by several suggested answers or completions. Select the one that BEST answers the question or completes the statement. *PRINT THE CORRECT ANSWER IN THE SPACE AT THE RIGHT.*

1. The army is BESEEJING the city. 1.____
   The word in capitals is misspelled. Write it correctly at the right.

2. Water AKYOOMYOOLATES in low places. 2.____
   The word in capitals is misspelled. Write it correctly at the right.

3. Moderate EKSURSYZ is healthful. 3.____
   The word in capitals is misspelled. Write it correctly at the right.

4. Eighteen percent of the mail carriers were off duty. There were 164 on duty. 4.____
   How many carriers were off duty?

5. MUSIC is to SOOTHING as NOISE is to 5.____

   A. waking   B. hearing   C. annoying
   D. toiling   E. sleeping

6. REWARD is to HERO as PUNISH is to 6.____

   A. good   B. ache   C. traitor
   D. everlasting E. wound

7. BOOK is to WRITER as STATUE is to 7.____

   A. sculptor   B. city   C. beauty
   D. picture   E. stone

8. To DECREASE is to 8.____

   A. grow   B. diminish C. settle
   D. decline   E. go

9. A HASTY person is 9.____

   A. deliberate B. meditative C. determined
   D. hurried   E. inaccurate

10. To DILATE is to 10.____

    A. contract B. degrade   C. expand
    D. lag   E. lose

11. *Enough is great riches.* 11.____
    The above quotation means MOST NEARLY

    A. no tent so good to live in as content
    B. make the best and leave the rest
    C. he is rich who does not want
    D. he is well paid who is well satisfied
    E. he who is bright is wealthy

30

12. *Good instruction is better than riches.* 12.____
    The above quotation means MOST NEARLY

    A. to keep from falling, keep climbing
    B. he who plants corn sows thistles
    C. there is no royal road to learning
    D. there is no wealth like unto knowledge
    E. he who is bright is wealthy

13. How old must a senator be? 13.____

    A. 21   B. 25   C. 30   D. 35   E. 32

14. A senator may hold his seat for 14.____

    A. limit of four terms   B. limit of six terms   C. limit of two terms
    D. no limited time   E. limit of six years

15. Who calls special sessions of Congress? 15.____

    A. The Cabinet   B. Congress
    C. Vice President   D. President
    E. Supreme Court

16. *A competitor's score on an examination may indicate that he possesses ability far superior to the demands of the position for which he has applied. Another competitor may rate below the passing mark on the same examination, and thereby appear to have inferior ability for this type of work, but even though he rates low, he may receive guidance from the civil service commission as to the positions for which he is qualified.* 16.____
    From the above paragraph, it is a known fact that all applicants

    A. rate high in the examination
    B. will receive the kind of position for which they are qualified
    C. benefit by the experience
    D. may learn their qualifications from their examination ratings
    E. rate low in the examination

17. I sold a house for $9,000 and received $1,200 as my share of the profits. My partner had invested 60% of the amount required to build the house, and I had invested 40%. How many dollars had I invested in the house? 17.____

18. It is FATEEGING to run fast. 18.____
    The word in capitals is misspelled. Write it correctly at the right.

19. Four ATURNEES appeared in court. 19.____
    The word in capitals is misspelled. Write it correctly at the right.

20. His illness at this time is REGRETUBUL. 20.____
    The word in capitals is misspelled. Write it correctly at the right.

KEY (CORRECT ANSWERS)

1. besieging
2. accumulates
3. exercise
4. 36
5. C

6. C
7. A
8. B
9. D
10. C

11. C
12. D
13. 30
14. D
15. D

16. D
17. $2400
18. fatiguing
19. attorneys
20. regrettable

EXAMINATION SECTION
TEST 1

DIRECTIONS: Each question or incomplete statement is followed by several suggested answers or completions. Select the one that BEST answers the question or completes the statement. *PRINT THE LETTER OF THE CORRECT ANSWER IN THE SPACE AT THE RIGHT.*

1. Add: 37.10
   .006
   300.105
   16.02
   7341.
   72.50

2. Add: 25 7/8
   31 3/4
   72 1/8
   96 1/2
   89 3/8

3. Multiply: .18902
   .018

4. Divide: .063)6048

5. To OSCILLATE means to
   A. quiver
   B. freeze
   C. swing back and forth
   D. hate
   E. rebound

6. *A New York broker who studied in Scotland during his younger years took a keen interest in the game of golf as it was played there. When he returned to the United States back in the seventies, he introduced the game over here by reproducing one of England's most famous courses.*
   According to the above paragraph, which one of the following statements is TRUE?
   A. Golf originated in the United States.
   B. The first golf course was built in England seventy years ago.
   C. Golf was introduced in the United States in the seventies.
   D. Golf was formerly played only by students.

7. CAT is to FELINE as COW is to
   A. quadruped
   B. pedigreed
   C. canine
   D. bovine
   E. equine

2 (#1)

8. BILL is to PAPER as COIN is to   8._____
    A. money   B. heavy   C. shiny   D. metal   E. round

9. WATER is to FLUID as IRON is to   9._____
    A. metal   B. rusty   C. solid   D. rails   E. mines

10. OVER is to UNDER as TRESTLE is to   10._____
    A. tunnel   B. bridge   C. trains
    D. skeleton   E. river

11. VAGUE means MOST NEARLY   11._____
    A. style   B. definite   C. not clear
    D. silly   E. tired

12. To AGGRAVATE is to   12._____
    A. indulge   B. counsel   C. inflate
    D. help   E. make worse

13. PRECISION means MOST NEARLY   13._____
    A. cutting   B. exactness   C. risky
    D. measurement E. training

14. A TERSE statement is   14._____
    A. long   B. condensed   C. rude
    D. wild   E. exact

15. A car will go 3/8 of a given distance in one hour.   15._____
What part will it cover in 5/8 of an hour?

16. An incubator was set with 120 eggs.   16._____
If 18 eggs failed to hatch, what percent hatched?

17. At $2.00 a case, what fraction of a case can be bought for 7/8 of a dollar?   17._____

18. A earns $3.50 a day. B earns ¼ more a day than A does.   18._____
How many days will it take B to earn the same amount that A earns in 10 days?

19. What is the postage on a package weighing 12 lbs., if the rate is 8 cents   19._____
for the first pound and 4 cents for each additional pound?

20. *Money order may be cashed without gain or profit by any post office having*   20._____
surplus money order funds.
What one word in the above sentence is synonymous to *excess*?

21. The jury AKWITED the prisoner.   21._____
The word in capitals is misspelled. Write it correctly at the right.

22. Dogs are SUGAYSHUS animals.   22._____
The word in capitals is misspelled. Write it correctly at the right.

3 (#1)

23. The parade caused a TRAFIK jam.
    The word in capitals is misspelled. Write it correctly at the right.
    23.____

24. The soldiers were ready to drop with FATEEG.
    The word in capitals is misspelled. Write it correctly at the right.
    24.____

25. To TOLERATE is to
    A. prohibit   B. spoil   C. endure
    D. liberate   E. rejoice
    25.____

KEY (CORRECT ANSWERS)

1.	7766.731	11.	C
2.	315 5/8	12.	E
3.	.00340236	13.	B
4.	9.6	14.	B
5.	C	15.	15/64
6.	C	16.	85%
7.	D	17.	7/16
8.	D	18.	8
9.	C	19.	52¢
10.	A	20.	surplus

21. acquitted
22. sagacious
23. traffic
24. fatigue
25. C

TEST 2

DIRECTIONS: Each question or incomplete statement is followed by several suggested answers or completions. Select the one that BEST answers the question or completes the statement. *PRINT THE LETTER OF THE CORRECT ANSWER IN THE SPACE AT THE RIGHT.*

1. To CONCUR means to
   - A. gather
   - B. repeat
   - C. assent
   - D. cause
   - E. put together

   1.____

2. *The world never knows its great men until it buries them* means MOST NEARLY
   - A. worry kills more men than work
   - B. when a thing is lost, its worth is known
   - C. every shoe fits not every foot
   - D. no man really lives who is buried in conceit

   2.____

3. *The Congress of the United States provided for the cooperation of the federal government with the states in the construction of rural roads all over the country and was a powerful force in the development of highways.*
   Judging from the above paragraph, which one of the following statements is TRUE?
   - A. Each state builds its highways and rural post roads unaided.
   - B. Congress builds all highways in the United States.
   - C. The state receive federal cooperation in the building of all roads.
   - D. The federal government assists in the building of post roads.

   2.____

4. LAKE is to LAND as ISLAND is to
   - A. separated
   - B. land
   - C. lonely
   - D. water
   - E. large

   4.____

5. NOVELIST is to FICTION as HISTORIAN is to
   - A. war
   - B. fact
   - C. books
   - D. school
   - E. primitive

   5.____

6. Four men agreed to dig a ditch in 20 days. After 10 days, only one-fourth of the ditch was completed.
   How many more men must be engaged to finish on time?

   6.____

7. *Let a man be true to his intentions and his efforts to fulfill them, and the point is gained, whether he succeed or not.*
   The above statement states that
   - A. a man cannot succeed unless he makes an effort to be true to his intentions
   - B. he may be satisfied with himself if he makes an effort to be true to his intentions
   - C. every point is gained whether a man succeeds or fails
   - D. no special effort is necessary for success
   - E. a certain amount of accomplishment always attends conscientious effort

   7.____

2 (#2)

8. MASS is to the WHOLE as ATOM is to 8.____
   A. physics B. weight C. solids D. part E. theory

9. DIME is to CENT a DOLLAR is to 9.____
   A. silver B. dime C. nickel D. paper E. coin

10. WISE is to FOOLISH as KNOWLEDGE is to 10.____
    A. simple B. ignorance C. books
    D. learned E. intolerance

11. REPUBLIC is to PRESIDENT as MONARCHY is to 11.____
    A. communists B. ruler C. constitution
    D. elections E. emperor

12. The distance from A to C is 423 miles. Tourists left A at 7 A.M. and traveled 12.____
    225 miles at 45 miles an hour, then stopped 30 minutes for lunch. The
    remainder of the trip was made at 36 miles an hour.
    At what time did they arrive at C?

13. The TRANSHENT population is quite large. 13.____
    The word in capitals is misspelled. Write it correctly at the right.

14. The LYOOTENANT wore a new uniform. 14.____
    The word in capitals is misspelled. Write it correctly at the right.

15. He stepped on the AKELURAYTER. 15.____
    The word in capitals is misspelled. Write it correctly at the right.

16. Paper is easily PUNGKTYOORD. 16.____
    The word in capitals is misspelled. Write it correctly at the right.

17. Even in hot weather, the water supply is ADEKWAYT. 17.____
    The word in capitals is misspelled. Write it correctly at the right.

18. PLAUSIBLE explanations are 18.____
    A. ample B. untrue C. courageous
    D. apparently right E. impossible

19. Which one of the following words may be applied to OPTION but not to 19.____
    PURCHASE or SALE?
    A. Legal B. Document C. Permanent
    D. Abstract E. Temporary F. Concession

20. ATTENTUATE means to 20.____
    A. wire B. flatter C. heed
    D. lessen E. be present F. extend

21. GIVING is to LENDING as TAKING is to
    A. alms B. prison C. thieves
    D. stealing E. kindness F. borrowing

21._____

22. A and B together earned $180.00 on piece work. B worked only 2/3 as fast as A, but he worked 6 days more and received $90.00.
    How many days did A work?

22._____

23. CHEAP is to ABUNDANT as COSTLY is to
    A. plenty B. inexpensive C. high priced
    D. scarce E. frugal

23._____

24. *Two-thirds of all American fires are home fires, and the preponderant cause is carelessness. This source of economic waste and human suffering can be checked only as we exercise greater care to eliminate such fire hazards as the accumulation of inflammable rubbish, careless smoking habits, overheated stoves, etc. Remember this, that even though you have no fire loss, you share in the loss of every fire in the country.*
    According to the above paragraph, which one of the following statements is TRUE?
    A. There are fewer fires in homes than in industrial plants.
    B. Fires are no loss when they are covered by insurance.
    C. This economic waste can be overcome only as we exercise greater care.
    D. Waste is the preponderant cause of home fires.
    E. Carelessness in the accumulation of rubbish causes fires.

24._____

25. If a stock of 500 rungs is divided into two parts, one of which contains 2/3 as many as the other, how many rugs are there in the smaller part?

25._____

KEY (CORRECT ANSWERS)

1. C
2. B
3. D
4. D
5. B

6. 8
7. E
8. D
9. B
10. B

11. E
12. 6:00 P.M
13. transient
14. lieutenant
15. accelerator

16. accumulated
17. adequate
18. D
19. E
20. D

21. F
22. 12
23. D
24. C
25. 200

TEST 3

DIRECTIONS: Each question or incomplete statement is followed by several suggested answers or completions. Select the one that BEST answers the question or completes the statement. *PRINT THE LETTER OF THE CORRECT ANSWER IN THE SPACE AT THE RIGHT.*

1. John travels a mile in 1/3 of an hour. Ben travels a mile in 3/10 of an hour. How many minutes does Ben finish before John, each traveling 12 miles?   1._____

2. KITTEN is to CAT as COLT is to   2._____
    A. young   B. pasture   C. horse
    D. donkey   E. cattle

3. WOLF is to HOWL as DOG is to   3._____
    A. bite   B. pet   C. bark
    D. pedigree   E. whine

4. DYNAMYT is used for blasting.   4._____
The word in capitals is misspelled. Write it correctly at the right.

5. The champion's OPOHNENT won the boxing match.   5._____
The word in capitals is misspelled. Write it correctly at the right.

6. The hungry man's appetite was APEEZD.   6._____
The word in capitals is misspelled. Write it correctly at the right.

7. WHEN is to WHERE as TIME is to   7._____
    A. hour   B. place   C. clock   D. here   E. work

8. ATLANTIC is to OCEAN as BRAZIL is to   8._____
    A. South America   B. country   C. river
    D. large   E. small

9. REGIMENT is to ARMY as SHIP is to   9._____
    A. marines   B. wars   C. navy
    D. submarine   E. commerce

10. *Substitute or temporary clerks shall be paid at the rate of $9.76 an hour for each hour or part hour after 6:00 P.M.*   10._____
What one word in the above quotation is synonymous to a fixed value?

11. *The United States leads the world in the amount of sugar consumed per capita, more than a hundred pounds annually for every person in the nation. The rest of the world is just as fond of sugar but not so able to buy it.*   11._____
Judging from the above paragraph, which one of the following statements is TRUE?

40

A. The United States leads in sugar production.
B. Europeans pay more for sugar.
C. Each person in the United States consumes a pound of sugar each week.
D. The per capita consumption of sugar in the United States is the largest in the world.
E. Americans are not so able to buy sugar as the rest of the world.
F. More sugar is consumed in the United States than in the rest of the world.

12. HABITUAL means MOST NEARLY 12.____
    A. healthy   B. customary   C. clothing
    D. harness   E. deadly

13. A COMPETENT man is one who is 13.____
    A. capable   B. clever   C. idle
    D. ambitious   E. punctual

14. To ADHERE is to 14.____
    A. hate   B. tape   C. degrade
    D. cling to   E. listen

15. To CALCULATE is to 15.____
    A. number   B. compute   C. whitewash
    D. tell tales   E. think

16. Which one of the following terms may be applied to MOTORCYCLE and AIRPLANE but not to BICYCLE? 16.____
    A. High speed   B. Padded seats   C. Metal
    D. Rubber tires   E. Two wheels

17. *He can who believes he can.* 17.____
    The above quotation means MOST NEARLY
    A. to believe a thing impossible is the way to make it go
    B. we are able when we feel so
    C. the man who believes is the man who achieves
    D. we walk by faith, not by sight
    E. nothing is impossible to him who tries

18. *How many acquaintances, but few friends.* 18.____
    The above quotation means MOST NEARLY
    A. be courteous to all, but intimate with few
    B. a true friend is forever a friend
    C. friends in distress make trouble less
    D. the only way to have a friend is to be one
    E. make friends of all you meet

19. *A man of many trades begs his bread on Sunday.*
    The above quotation means MOST NEARLY
    A. with too many irons in the fire some will burn
    B. doing everything is doing nothing
    C. one cannot do many things profitably at the same time
    D. an intense hour will do more than two dreamy years
    E. A man without a trade will beg his bread

20. *Caution is the parent of safety.*
    The above quotation means MOST NEARLY
    A. all things belong to the prudent
    B. better a mistake avoided than two corrected
    C. look before you leap
    D. better go around than jump and fall short

19.____

20.____

KEY (CORRECT ANSWERS)

1.	24 min.	11.	D
2.	C	12.	B
3.	C	13.	A
4.	dynamite	14.	D
5.	opponent	15.	B
6.	appeased	16.	A
7.	B	17.	C
8.	B	18.	A
9.	C	19.	C
10.	rate	20.	D

READING COMPREHENSION
UNDERSTANDING AND INTERPRETING WRITTEN MATERIAL
EXAMINATION SECTION
TEST 1

DIRECTIONS: Each question or incomplete statement is followed by several suggested answers or completions. Select the one that BEST answers the question or completes the statement. *PRINT THE LETTER OF THE CORRECT ANSWER IN THE SPACE AT THE RIGHT.*

Questions 1-8.

DIRECTIONS: Questions 1 through 8 are to be answered on the basis of the following regulations governing Newspaper Carriers when on subway trains or station platforms. These Newspaper Carriers are issued badges which entitle them to enter subway stations, when carrying papers in accordance with these regulations, without paying a fare.

REGULATIONS GOVERNING NEWSPAPER CARRIERS WHEN ON SUBWAY TRAINS OR STATION PLATFORMS

1. Carriers must wear badges at all times when on trains.
2. Carriers must not sort, separate, or wrap bundles on trains or insert sections.
3. Carriers must not obstruct platform of cars or stations.
4. Carriers may make delivery to stands inside the stations by depositing their badge with the station agent.
5. Throwing of bundles is strictly prohibited and will be cause for arrest.
6. Each bundle must not be over 18" x 12" x 15".
7. Not more than two bundles shall be carried by each carrier. (An extra fare to be charged for a second bundle.)
8. No wire to be used on bundles carried into stations.

1. These regulations do NOT prohibit carriers on trains from _____ newspapers.　　1.____

   A. sorting bundles of　　　　　　B. carrying bundles of
   C. wrapping bundles of　　　　　D. inserting sections into

2. A carrier delivering newspapers to a stand inside of the station MUST　　2.____

   A. wear his badge at all times
   B. leave his badge with the railroad clerk
   C. show his badge to the railroad clerk
   D. show his badge at the newsstand

3. Carriers are warned against throwing bundles of newspapers from trains MAINLY because these acts may　　3.____

   A. wreck the stand　　　　　　B. cause injury to passengers
   C. hurt the carrier　　　　　　　D. damage the newspaper

4. It is permissible for a carrier to temporarily leave his bundles of newspapers 4.____

   A. near the subway car's door
   B. at the foot of the station stairs
   C. in front of the exit gate
   D. on a station bench

5. Of the following, the carrier who should NOT be restricted from entering the subway is 5.____
   the one carrying a bundle which is _____ long, _____ wide, and _____ high.

   A. 15"; 18"; 18"   B. 18"; 12"; 18"
   C. 18"; 12"; 15"   D. 18"; 15"; 15"

6. A carrier who will have to pay one fare is carrying _____ bundle(s). 6.____

   A. one   B. two   C. three   D. four

7. Wire may NOT be used for tying bundles because it may be 7.____

   A. rusty
   B. expensive
   C. needed for other purposes
   D. dangerous to other passengers

8. If a carrier is arrested in violation of these regulations, the PROBABLE reason is that he 8.____

   A. carried too many papers
   B. was not wearing his badge
   C. separated bundles of newspapers on the train
   D. tossed a bundle of newspapers to a carrier on a train

Questions 9-12.

DIRECTIONS: Questions 9 through 12 are to be answered on the basis of the Bulletin printed below. Read this Bulletin carefully before answering these questions. Select your answers ONLY on the basis of this Bulletin.

BULLETIN

Rule 107(m) states, in part, that *Before closing doors they (Conductors) must afford passengers an opportunity to detrain and entrain...*

Doors must be left open long enough to allow passengers to enter and exit from the train. Closing doors on passengers too quickly does not help to shorten the station stop and is a violation of the safety and courtesy which must be accorded to all our passengers.

The proper and effective way to keep passengers moving in and out of the train is to use the public address system. When the train is excessively crowded and passengers on the platform are pushing those in the cars, it may be necessary to close the doors after a reasonable period of time has been allowed.

Closing doors on passengers too quickly is a violation of rules and will be cause for disciplinary actions.

9. Which of the following statements is CORRECT about closing doors on passengers too quickly? It

   A. will shorten the running time from terminal to terminal
   B. shortens the station stop but is a violation of safety and courtesy
   C. does not help shorten the station stop time
   D. makes the passengers detrain and entrain quicker

10. The BEST way to get passengers to move in and out of cars quickly is to

    A. have the platform conductors urge passengers to move into doorways
    B. make announcements over the public address system
    C. start closing doors while passengers are getting on
    D. set a fixed time for stopping at each station

11. The conductor should leave doors open at each station stop long enough for passengers to

    A. squeeze into an excessively crowded train
    B. get from the local to the express train
    C. get off and get on the train
    D. hear the announcements over the public address system

12. Closing doors on passengers too quickly is a violation of rules and is cause for

    A. the conductor's immediate suspension
    B. the conductor to be sent back to the terminal for another assignment
    C. removal of the conductor at the next station
    D. disciplinary action to be taken against the conductor

Questions 13-15.

DIRECTIONS: Questions 13 through 15 are to be answered on the basis of the Bulletin printed below. Read this Bulletin carefully before answering these questions. Select your answers ONLY on the basis of this Bulletin.

BULLETIN

Conductors assigned to train service are not required to wear uniform caps from June 1 to September 30, inclusive.

Conductors assigned to platform duty are required to wear the uniform cap at all times. Conductors are reminded that they must furnish their badge numbers to anyone who requests same.

During the above-mentioned period, conductors may remove their uniform coats. The regulation summer short-sleeved shirts must be worn with the regulation uniform trousers. Suspenders are not permitted if the uniform coat is removed. Shoes are to be black but sandals, sneakers, suede, canvas, or two-tone footwear must not be worn.

Conductors may work without uniform tie if the uniform coat is removed. However, only the top collar button may be opened. The tie may not be removed if the uniform coat is worn.

13. Conductors assigned to platform duty are required to wear uniform caps

    A. at all times except from June 1 to September 30, inclusive
    B. whenever they are on duty
    C. only from June 1 to September 30, inclusive
    D. only when they remove their uniform coats

14. Suspenders are permitted ONLY if conductors wear

    A. summer short-sleeved shirts with uniform trousers
    B. uniform trousers without belt loops
    C. the type permitted by the authority
    D. uniform coats

15. A conductor MUST furnish his badge number to

    A. authority supervisors only
    B. members of special inspection only
    C. anyone who asks him for it
    D. passengers only

Questions 16-17.

DIRECTIONS: Questions 16 and 17 are to be answered SOLELY on the basis of the following Bulletin.

BULLETIN

Effective immediately, Conductors on trains equipped with public address systems shall make the following announcements in addition to their regular station announcement. At stations where passengers normally board trains from their homes or places of employment, the announcement shall be *Good Morning* or *Good Afternoon* or *Good Evening*, depending on the time of the day. At stations where passengers normally leave trains for their homes or places of employment, the announcement shall be *Have a Good Day* or *Good Night*, depending on the time of day or night.

16. The MAIN purpose of making the additional announcements mentioned in the Bulletin is MOST likely to

    A. keep passengers informed about the time of day
    B. determine whether the public address system works in case of an emergency
    C. make the passengers' ride more pleasant
    D. have the conductor get used to using the public address system

17. According to this Bulletin, a conductor should greet passengers boarding the D train at the Coney Island Station at 8 A.M. Monday by announcing

    A. Have a Good Day
    B. Good Morning
    C. Watch your step as you leave
    D. Good Evening

Questions 18-25.

DIRECTIONS: Questions 18 through 25 are to be answered on the basis of the information regarding the incident given below. Read this information carefully before answering these questions.

INCIDENT

As John Brown, a cleaner, was sweeping the subway station platform, in accordance with his assigned schedule, he was accused by Henry Adams of unnecessarily bumping him with the broom and scolded for doing this work when so many passengers were on the platform. Adams obtained Brown's badge number and stated that he would report the matter to the Transit Authority. Standing around and watching this were Mary Smith, a schoolteacher, Ann Jones, a student, and Joe Black, a maintainer, with Jim Roe, his helper, who had been working on one of the turnstiles. Brown thereupon proceeded to take the names and addresses of these people as required by the Transit Authority rule which directs that names and addresses of as many disinterested witnesses be taken as possible. Shortly thereafter, a train arrived at the station and Adams, as well as several other people, boarded the train and left. Brown went back to his work of sweeping the station.

18. The cleaner was sweeping the station at this time because
    A. the platform was unusually dirty
    B. there were very few passengers on the platform
    C. he had no regard for the passengers
    D. it was set by his work schedule

19. This incident proves that
    A. witnesses are needed in such cases
    B. porters are generally careless
    C. subway employees stick together
    D. brooms are dangerous in the subway

20. Joe Black was a
    A. helper   B. maintainer
    C. cleaner   D. teacher

21. The number of persons witnessing this incident was
    A. 2   B. 3   C. 4   D. 5

22. The addresses of witnesses are required so that they may later be
    A. depended on to testify   B. recognized
    C. paid   D. located

23. The person who said he would report this incident to the transit authority was
    A. Black   B. Adams   C. Brown   D. Roe

24. The ONLY person of the following who positively did NOT board the train was

    A. Brown   B. Smith   C. Adams   D. Jones

25. As a result of this incident,

    A. no action need be taken against the cleaner unless Adams makes a written complaint
    B. the cleaner should be given the rest of the day off
    C. the handles of the brooms used should be made shorter
    D. Brown's badge number should be changed

KEY (CORRECT ANSWERS)

1.	B	11.	C
2.	B	12.	D
3.	B	13.	B
4.	D	14.	D
5.	C	15.	C
6.	A	16.	C
7.	D	17.	B
8.	D	18.	D
9.	C	19.	A
10.	B	20.	B

21. C
22. D
23. B
24. A
25. A

TEST 2

DIRECTIONS: Each question or incomplete statement is followed by several suggested answers or completions. Select the one that BEST answers the question or completes the statement. *PRINT THE LETTER OF THE CORRECT ANSWER IN THE SPACE AT THE RIGHT.*

Questions 1-10.

DIRECTIONS: Questions 1 through 10 are to be answered on the basis of the information contained in the following safety rules. Read the rules carefully before answering these questions.

SAFETY RULES

Employees must take every precaution to prevent accidents, or injury to persons, or damage to property. For this reason, they must observe conditions of the equipment and tools with which they work, and the structures upon which they work.

It is the duty of all employees to report to their superior all dangerous conditions which they may observe. Employees must use every precaution to prevent the origin of fire. If they discover smoke or a fire in the subway, they shall proceed to the nearest telephone and notify the trainmaster giving their name, badge number, and location of the trouble.

In case of accidents on the subway system, employees must, if possible, secure the name, address, and telephone number of any passengers who may have been injured.

Employees at or near the location of trouble on the subway system, whether it be a fire or an accident, shall render all practical assistance which they are qualified to perform.

1. The BEST way for employees to prevent an accident is to 1.____

   A. secure the names of the injured persons
   B. arrive promptly at the location of the accident
   C. give their name and badge numbers to the trainmaster
   D. take all necessary precautions

2. In case of trouble, trackmen are NOT expected to 2.____

   A. report fires
   B. give help if they don't know how
   C. secure telephone numbers of persons injured in subway accidents
   D. give their badge number to anyone

3. Trackmen MUST 3.____

   A. be present at all fires
   B. see all accidents
   C. report dangerous conditions
   D. be the first to discover smoke in the subway

4. Observing conditions means to

   A. look at things carefully
   B. report what you see
   C. ignore things that are none of your business
   D. correct dangerous conditions

5. A dangerous condition existing on the subway system which a trackman should observe and report to his superior would be

   A. passengers crowding into trains
   B. trains running behind schedule
   C. tools in defective condition
   D. some newspapers on the track

6. If a trackman discovers a badly worn rail, he should

   A. not take any action
   B. remove the worn section of rail
   C. notify his superior
   D. replace the rail

7. The MAIN reason a trackman should observe the condition of his tools is

   A. so that they won't be stolen
   B. because they don't belong to him
   C. to prevent accidents
   D. because they cannot be replaced

8. If a passenger who paid his fare is injured in a subway accident, it is MOST important that an employee obtain the passenger's

   A. name
   B. age
   C. badge number
   D. destination

9. An employee who happens to be at the scene of an accident on a crowded station of the system should

   A. not give assistance unless he chooses to do so
   B. leave the scene immediately
   C. question all bystanders
   D. render whatever assistance he can

10. If a trackman discovers a fire at one end of a station platform and telephones the information to the trainmaster, he need NOT give

    A. the trainmaster's name
    B. the name of the station involved
    C. his own name
    D. the number of his badge

Questions 11-15.

DIRECTIONS: Questions 11 through 15 are to be answered on the basis of the information contained in the safety regulations given below. Refer to these rules in answering these questions.

REGULATIONS FOR SMALL GROUPS WHO MOVE FROM POINT TO POINT ON THE TRACKS

Employees who perform duties on the tracks in small groups and who move from point to point along the trainway must be on the alert at all times and prepared to clear the track when a train approaches without unnecessarily slowing it down. Underground at all times, and out-of-doors between sunset and sunrise, such employees must not enter upon the tracks unless each of them is equipped with an approved light. Flashlights must not be used for protection by such groups. Upon clearing the track to permit a train to pass, each member of the group must give a proceed signal, by hand or light, to the motorman of the train. Whenever such small groups are working in an area protected by caution lights or flags, but are not members of the gang for whom the flagging protection was established, they must not give proceed signals to motormen. The purpose of this rule is to avoid a motorman's confusing such signal with that of the flagman who is protecting a gang. Whenever a small group is engaged in work of an engrossing nature or at any time when the view of approaching trains is limited by reason of curves or otherwise, one man of the group, equipped with a whistle, must be assigned properly to warn and protect the man or men at work and must not perform any other duties while so assigned.

11. If a small group of men are traveling along the tracks toward their work location and a train approaches, they should

    A. stop the train
    B. signal the motorman to go slowly
    C. clear the track
    D. stop immediately

12. Small groups may enter upon the tracks

    A. only between sunset and sunrise
    B. provided each has an approved light
    C. provided their foreman has a good flashlight
    D. provided each man has an approved flashlight

13. After a small group has cleared the tracks in an area unprotected by caution lights or flags,

    A. each member must give the proceed signal to the motorman
    B. the foreman signals the motorman to proceed
    C. the motorman can proceed provided he goes slowly
    D. the last member off the tracks gives the signal to the motorman

14. If a small group is working in an area protected by the signals of a track gang, the members of the small group

    A. need not be concerned with train movement
    B. must give the proceed signal together with the track gang

    C. can delegate one of their members to give the proceed signal
    D. must not give the proceed signal

15. If the view of approaching trains is blocked, the small group should

    A. move to where they can see the trains
    B. delegate one of the group to warn and protect them
    C. keep their ears alert for approaching trains
    D. refuse to work at such locations

Questions 16-25.

DIRECTIONS: Questions 16 through 25 are to be answered SOLELY on the basis of the article about general safety precautions given below.

GENERAL SAFETY PRECAUTIONS

When work is being done on or next to a track on which regular trains are running, special signals must be displayed as called for in the general rules for flagging. Yellow caution signals, green clear signals, and a flagman with a red danger signal are required for the protection of traffic and workmen in accordance with the standard flagging rules. The flagman shall also carry a white signal for display to the motorman when he may proceed. The foreman in charge must see that proper signals are displayed.

On elevated lines during daylight hours, the yellow signal shall be a yellow flag, the red signal shall be a red flag, the green signal shall be a green flag, and the white signal shall be a white flag. In subway sections, and on elevated lines after dark, the yellow signal shall be a yellow lantern, the red signal shall be a red lantern, the green signal shall be a green lantern, and the white signal shall be a white lantern.

Caution and clear signals are to be secured to the elevated or subway structure with non-metallic fastenings outside the clearance line of the train and on the motorman's side of the track.

16. On elevated lines during daylight hours, the caution signal is a

    A. yellow lantern   B. green lantern
    C. yellow flag   D. green flag

17. In subway sections, the clear signal is a

    A. yellow lantern   B. green lantern
    C. yellow flag   D. green flag

18. The MINIMUM number of lanterns that a subway track flagman should carry is

    A. 1   B. 2   C. 3   D. 4

19. The PRIMARY purpose of flagging is to protect the

    A. flagman   B. motorman
    C. track workers   D. railroad

20. A suitable fastening for securing caution lights to the elevated or subway structure is 20.____
    A. copper nails   B. steel wire
    C. brass rods   D. cotton twine

21. On elevated structures during daylight hours, the red flag is held by the 21.____
    A. motorman   B. foreman   C. trackman   D. flagman

22. The signal used in the subway to notify a motorman to proceed is a 22.____
    A. white lantern   B. green lantern
    C. red flag   D. yellow flag

23. The caution, clear, and danger signals are displayed for the information of 23.____
    A. trackmen   B. workmen   C. flagmen   D. motormen

24. Since the motorman's cab is on the right-hand side, caution signals should be secured to the 24.____
    A. right-hand running rail
    B. left-hand running rail
    C. structure to the right of the track
    D. structure to the left of the track

25. In a track work gang, the person responsible for the proper display of signals is the 25.____
    A. track worker   B. foreman
    C. motorman   D. flagman

KEY (CORRECT ANSWERS)

1. D   11. C
2. B   12. B
3. C   13. A
4. A   14. D
5. C   15. B

6. C   16. C
7. C   17. B
8. A   18. B
9. D   19. C
10. A   20. D

21. D
22. A
23. D
24. C
25. B

TEST 3

DIRECTIONS: Each question or incomplete statement is followed by several suggested answers or completions. Select the one that BEST answers the question or completes the statement. *PRINT THE LETTER OF THE CORRECT ANSWER IN THE SPACE AT THE RIGHT.*

Questions 1-6.

DIRECTIONS: Questions 1 through 6 are to be answered on the basis of the Bulletin Order given below. Refer to this bulletin when answering these questions.

BULLETIN ORDER NO. 67

SUBJECT: Procedure for Handling Fire Occurrences

In order that the Fire Department may be notified of all fires, even those that have been extinguished by our own employees, any employee having knowledge of a fire must notify the Station Department Office immediately on telephone extensions D-4177, D-4181, D-4185, or D-4189.

Specific information regarding the fire should include the location of the fire, the approximate distance north or south of the nearest station, and the track designation, line, and division.

In addition, the report should contain information as to the status of the fire and whether our forces have extinguished it or if Fire Department equipment is required.

When all information has been obtained, the Station Supervisor in Charge in the Station Department Office will notify the Desk Trainmaster of the Division involved.

Richard Roe,
Superintendent

1. An employee having knowledge of a fire should FIRST notify the

   A. Station Department Office
   B. Fire Department
   C. Desk Trainmaster
   D. Station Supervisor

2. If bulletin order number 1 was issued on January 2, bulletins are being issued at the monthly average of

   A. 8 B. 10 C. 12 D. 14

3. It is clear from the bulletin that

   A. employees are expected to be expert fire fighters
   B. many fires occur on the transit system
   C. train service is usually suspended whenever a fire occurs
   D. some fires are extinguished without the help of the Fire Department

4. From the information furnished in this bulletin, it can be assumed that the

   A. Station Department office handles a considerable number of telephone calls
   B. Superintendent Investigates the handling of all subway fires
   C. Fire Department is notified only in ease of large fires
   D. employee first having knowledge of the fire must call all 4 extensions

5. The PROBABLE reason for notifying the Fire Department even when the fire has been extinguished by a subway employee is because the Fire Department is

   A. a city agency
   B. still responsible to check the fire
   C. concerned with fire prevention
   D. required to clean up after the fire

6. Information about the fire NOT specifically required is

   A. track   B. time of day   C. station   D. division

Questions 7-10.

DIRECTIONS: Questions 7 through 10 are to be answered on the basis of the paragraph on fire fighting shown below. When answering these questions, refer to this paragraph.

FIRE FIGHTING

A security officer should remember the cardinal rule that water or soda acid fire extinguishers should not be used on any electrical fire, and apply it in the case of a fire near the third rail. In addition, security officers should familiarize themselves with all available fire alarms and fire-fighting equipment within their assigned posts. Use of the fire alarm should bring responding Fire Department apparatus quickly to the scene. Familiarity with the fire-fighting equipment near his post would help in putting out incipient fires. Any man calling for the Fire Department should remain outside so that he can direct the Fire Department to the fire. As soon as possible thereafter, the special inspection desk must be notified, and a complete written report of the fire, no matter how small, must be submitted to this office. The security officer must give the exact time and place it started, who discovered it, how it was extinguished, the damage done, cause of same, list of any injured persons with the extent of their injuries, and the name of the Fire Chief in charge. All defects noticed by the security officer concerning the fire alarm or any fire-fighting equipment must be reported to the special inspection department.

7. It would be PROPER to use water to put out a fire in a(n)

   A. electric motor
   B. electric switch box
   C. waste paper trash can
   D. electric generator

8. After calling the Fire Department from a street box to report a fire, the security officer should then

   A. return to the fire and help put it out
   B. stay outside and direct the Fire Department to the fire
   C. find a phone and call his boss
   D. write out a report for the special inspection desk

9. A security officer is required to submit a complete written report of a fire 9._____

   A. two weeks after the fire
   B. the day following the fire
   C. as soon as possible
   D. at his convenience

10. In his report of a fire, it is NOT necessary for the security officer to state 10._____

    A. time and place of the fire
    B. who discovered the fire
    C. the names of persons injured
    D. quantity of Fire Department equipment used

Questions 11-16.

DIRECTIONS: Questions 11 through 16 are to be answered on the basis of the Notice given below. Refer to this Notice in answering these questions.

NOTICE

Your attention is called to Route Request Buttons that are installed on all new type Interlocking Home Signals where there is a choice of route in the midtown area. The route request button is to be operated by the motorman when the home signal is at danger and no call-on is displayed or when improper route is displayed.

To operate, the motorman will press the button for the desiredroute as indicated under each button; a light will then go on over the buttons to inform the motorman that his request has been registered in the tower.

If the towerman desires to give the motorman a route other than the one he selected, the towerman will cancel out the light over the route selection buttons. The motorman will then accept the route given.

If no route or call-on is given, the motorman will sound his whistle for the signal maintainer, secure his train, and call the desk trainmaster.

11. The official titles of the two classes of employee whose actions would MOST frequently be affected by the contents of this notice are 11._____

    A. motorman and trainmaster
    B. signal maintainer and trainmaster
    C. towerman and motorman
    D. signal maintainer and towerman

12. A motorman should use a route request button when 12._____

    A. the signal indicates proceed on main line
    B. a call-on is displayed
    C. the signal indicates stop
    D. the signal indicates proceed on diverging route

13. The PROPER way to request a route is to 13.____
    A. press the button corresponding to the desired route
    B. press the button a number of times to correspond with the number of the route requested
    C. stop at the signal and blow four short blasts
    D. stop at the signal and telephone the tower

14. The motorman will know that his requested route has been registered in the tower if 14.____
    A. a light comes on over the route request buttons
    B. an acknowledging signal is sounded on the tower horn
    C. the light in the route request button goes dark
    D. the home signal continues to indicate stop

15. Under certain conditions, when stopped at such home signal, the motorman must signal 15.____
    for a signal maintainer and call the desk trainmaster.
    Such condition exists when, after standing awhile,
    A. the towerman continues to give the wrong route
    B. the towerman does not acknowledge the signal
    C. no route or call-on is given
    D. the light over the route request buttons is cancelled out

16. It is clear that route request buttons 16.____
    A. eliminate train delays due to signals at junctions
    B. keep the towerman alert
    C. force motormen and towermen to be more careful
    D. are a more accurate form of communication than the whistle.

Questions 17-22.

DIRECTIONS: Questions 17 through 22 are to be answered on the basis of the instructions for removal of paper given below. Read these instructions carefully before answering these questions.

GENERAL INSTRUCTIONS FOR REMOVAL OF PAPER

When a cleaner's work schedule calls for the bagging of paper, he will remove paper from the waste paper receptacles, bag it, and place the bags at the head end of the platform, where they will be picked up by the work train. He will fill bags with paper to a weight that can be carried without danger of personal injury, as porters are forbidden to drag bags of paper over the platform. Cleaners are responsible that all bags of paper are arranged so as to prevent their falling from the platform to tracks, and so as to not interfere with passenger traffic.

17. A GOOD reason for removing the paper from receptacles and placing it in bags is that 17.____
    bags are more easily
    A. stored   B. weighed   C. handled   D. emptied

18. The *head end* of a local station platform is the end   18.____

    A. in the direction that trains are running
    B. nearest to which the trains stop
    C. where there is an underpass to the other side
    D. at which the change booth is located

19. The MOST likely reason for having the filled bags placed at the head end of the station rather than at the other end is that   19.____

    A. a special storage space is provided there for them
    B. this end of the platform is farthest from the passengers
    C. most porters' closets are located near the head end
    D. the work train stops at this end to pick them up

20. Limiting the weight to which the bags can be filled is PROBABLY done to   20.____

    A. avoid having too many ripped or broken bags
    B. protect the porter against possible rupture
    C. make sure that all bags are filled fairly evenly
    D. insure that, when stored, the bags will not fall to the track

21. The MOST important reason for not allowing filled bags to be dragged over the platform is that the bags   21.____

    A. could otherwise be loaded too heavily
    B. might leave streaks on the platform
    C. would wear out too quickly
    D. might spill paper on the platform

22. The instructions do NOT hold a porter responsible for a bag of paper which   22.____

    A. is torn due to dragging over a platform
    B. falls on a passenger because it was poorly stacked
    C. falls to the track without being pushed
    D. is ripped open by school children

Questions 23-25.

DIRECTIONS: Questions 23 through 25 are to be answered on the basis of the situation described below. Consider the facts given in this situation when answering these questions.

SITUATION

A new detergent that is to be added to water and the resulting mixture just wiped on any surface has been tested by the station department and appeared to be excellent. However, you notice, after inspecting a large number of stations that your porters have cleaned with this detergent, that the surfaces cleaned are not as clean as they formerly were when the old method was used.

23. The MAIN reason for the station department testing the new detergent in the first place was to make certain that   23.____

    A. it was very simple to use
    B. a little bit would go a long way
    C. there was no stronger detergent on the market
    D. it was superior to anything formerly used

24. The MAIN reason that such a poor cleaning job resulted was MOST likely due to the   24.____

    A. porters being lax on the job
    B. detergent not being as good as expected
    C. incorrect amount of water being mixed with the detergent
    D. fact that the surfaces cleaned needed to be scrubbed

25. The reason for inspecting a number of stations was to   25.____

    A. determine whether all porters did the same job
    B. insure that the result of the cleaning job was the same in each location
    C. be certain that the detergent was used in each station inspected
    D. see whether certain surfaces cleaned better than others

---

KEY (CORRECT ANSWERS)

1.	A	11.	C
2.	C	12.	C
3.	D	13.	A
4.	A	14.	A
5.	C	15.	C
6.	B	16.	D
7.	C	17.	C
8.	B	18.	A
9.	C	19.	D
10.	D	20.	B

21.	C
22.	D
23.	D
24.	B
25.	B

WORD MEANING

EXAMINATION SECTION
TEST 1

DIRECTIONS: For the following questions, select the word or group of words lettered A, B, C, D, or E that means MOST NEARLY the same as the word in capital letters. *PRINT THE LETTER OF THE CORRECT ANSWER IN THE SPACE AT THE RIGHT.*

1. RENDEZVOUS means *most nearly*
   - A. parade
   - B. neighborhood
   - C. saloon
   - D. wander about
   - E. meeting place

2. EMINENT means *most nearly*
   - A. noted
   - B. rich
   - C. rounded
   - D. nearby
   - E. mindful

3. CAUSTIC means *most nearly*
   - A. cheap
   - B. sweet
   - C. evil
   - D. sharp
   - E. costly

4. To BARTER means *most nearly* to
   - A. annoy
   - B. trade
   - C. argue
   - D. cheat
   - E. rotate

5. APTITUDE means *most nearly*
   - A. friendliness
   - B. talent
   - C. conceit
   - D. generosity
   - E. interest

6. To PROTRUDE means *most nearly* to
   - A. project
   - B. defend
   - C. choke
   - D. boast
   - E. intrude

7. FORTITUDE means *most nearly*
   - A. disposition
   - B. restlessness
   - C. courage
   - D. poverty
   - E. strength

8. PRELUDE means *most nearly*
   - A. introduction
   - B. meaning
   - C. prayer
   - D. secret
   - E. pretense

9. SECLUSION means *most nearly*
   - A. primitive
   - B. influence
   - C. imagination
   - D. privacy
   - E. deceit

10. To RECTIFY means *most nearly* to
    - A. terrify
    - B. construct
    - C. divide
    - D. scold
    - E. correct

11. To TRAVERSE means *most nearly* to
    - A. rotate
    - B. compose
    - C. train
    - D. cross
    - E. oppose

12. To ALLEGE means *most nearly* to 12.____
    A. raise   B. convict   C. declare   D. chase   E. confuse

13. MENIAL means *most nearly* 13.____
    A. pleasant   B. unselfish   C. humble   D. stupid   E. mean

14. To DEPLETE means *most nearly* to 14.____
    A. exhaust   B. gather   C. repay   D. close   E. deny

15. To ERADICATE means *most nearly* to 15.____
    A. construct   B. advise   C. destroy   D. exclaim   E. indicate

16. To CAPITULATE means *most nearly* to 16.____
    A. cover   B. surrender   C. receive   D. execute   E. command

17. To RESTRAIN means *most nearly* to 17.____
    A. restore   B. drive   C. review   D. limit   E. detain

18. To AMALGAMATE means *most nearly* to 18.____
    A. join   B. force   C. correct   D. clash   E. amend

19. DEJECTED means *most nearly* 19.____
    A. beaten   B. speechless   C. weak   D. low-spirited   E. erect

20. To DETAIN means *most nearly* to 20.____
    A. hide   B. accuse   C. hold   D. mislead   E. complain

KEYS (CORRECT ANSWERS)

1.	E	6.	A	11.	D	16.	B
2.	A	7.	C	12.	C	17.	D
3.	D	8.	A	13.	C	18.	A
4.	B	9.	D	14.	A	19.	D
5.	B	10.	E	15.	C	20.	C

TEST 2

DIRECTIONS: For the following questions, select the word or group of words lettered A, B, C, D, or E that means MOST NEARLY the same as the word in capital letters. *PRINT THE LETTER OF THE CORRECT ANSWER IN THE SPACE AT THE RIGHT.*

1. CONCEPT means *most nearly*   1.____
   A. conclusion   B. purpose   C. thought   D. example   E. conspiracy

2. ADROIT means *most nearly*   2.____
   A. skillful   B. informed   C. secretive   D. polite   E. aged

3. CENSURE means *most nearly*   3.____
   A. acclaim   B. criticize   C. enumerate   D. examine   E. insure

4. COHERENT means *most nearly*   4.____
   A. interesting   B. contradictory   C. logically consistent
   D. fully conscious   E. uncertain

5. To PROCRASTINATE means *most nearly* to   5.____
   A. delay action   B. predict an occurrence   C. accomplish
   D. support   E. lament

6. LATENT means *most nearly*   6.____
   A. restrictive   B. forcible   C. deplorable   D. hidden   E. overt

7. ACUMEN means *most nearly*   7.____
   A. asset   B. keenness   C. disability   D. power   E. agility

8. DECORUM means *most nearly*   8.____
   A. ornament   B. improvement   C. distinction
   D. orderliness   E. derision

9. CREDIBLE means *most nearly*   9.____
   A. repetitive   B. believable   C. praiseworthy
   D. stimulating   E. credulous

10. RAMIFICATION means *most nearly*   10.____
    A. outgrowth   B. obstacle   C. unfair advantage
    D. cause for alarm   E. horn

11. PARAMOUNT means *most nearly*   11.____
    A. proud   B. supreme   C. recent   D. well-known   E. parallel

12. DUPLICITY means *most nearly*   12.____
    A. brilliance   B. imitation   C. deception   D. anxiety   E. despair

13. To ABSOLVE means *most nearly* to

    A. punish B. attribute C. accept D. acquit E. abstain

14. To REPUDIATE means *most nearly* to

    A. remember B. reveal C. renounce D. admire E. repulse

15. COERCION means *most nearly*

    A. caution
    B. intention
    C. disagreeent
    D. compulsion
    E. opinion

16. PERTINENT means *most nearly*

    A. insolent B. attractive C. appropriate D. conclusive E. potent

17. COGNIZANT means *most nearly*

    A. opposed B. aware C. deserving D. critical E. related

18. To ADVOCATE means *most nearly* to

    A. display B. abhor C. object D. offend E. support

19. To VERIFY means *most nearly* to

    A. challenge B. change C. revere D. reveal E. confirm

20. INSIGNIFICANT means *most nearly*

    A. incorrect B. limited C. unimportant D. undesirable E. unpleasant

KEYS (CORRECT ANSWERS)

1. C	6. D	11. B	16. C
2. A	7. B	12. C	17. B
3. E	8. D	13. D	18. E
4. C	9. B	14. C	19. E
5. A	10. A	15. D	20. C

TEST 3

DIRECTIONS: For the following questions, select the word or group of words lettered A, B, C, D, or E that means MOST NEARLY the same as the word in capital letters. *PRINT THE LETTER OF THE CORRECT ANSWER IN THE SPACE AT THE RIGHT.*

1. AMBIGUOUS means *most nearly*
   A. separate   B. uncertain   C. improper   D. lengthy   E. avid

   1._____

2. To INSTIGATE means *most nearly* to
   A. insult   B. find fault with   C. provoke
   D. examine closely   E. instill

   2._____

3. RATIONAL means *most nearly*
   A. raucous   B. rapid   C. meager   D. impartial   E. sensible

   3._____

4. To AFFILIATE means *most nearly* to
   A. afford   B. respect   C. complicate   D. join   E. infiltrate

   4._____

5. To IMPROVISE means *most nearly* to
   A. account for   B. show conclusively   C. invent offhand
   D. slow down   E. improve

   5._____

6. DUBIOUS means *most nearly*
   A. doubtful   B. uninterested
   C. duplicate   D. ignorant
   E. docile

   6._____

7. To ABRIDGE means *most nearly* to
   A. apply   B. shorten   C. adjust   D. reach   E. apply

   7._____

8. To COMPRISE means *most nearly* to
   A. settle   B. be unaware of   C. require
   D. consist of   E. consider

   8._____

9. To INGRATIATE means *most nearly* to
   A. resent   B. show lack of appreciation
   C. bring into favor   D. lower   E. frustrate

   9._____

10. TENACIOUS means *most nearly*
    A. unyielding   B. anxious   C. cruel   D. vague   E. tenuous

    10._____

11. To ALLEVIATE means *most nearly* to
    A. avoid   B. relieve   C. allow   D. disagree   E. allude

    11._____

12. ZEALOUS means *most nearly*

    A. unselfish
    B. suspicious
    C. enthusiastic
    D. harsh
    E. jealous

13. To DISSEMINATE means *most nearly* to

    A. copy   B. discuss   C. confirm   D. spread   E. disdain

14. To INNOVATE means *most nearly* to

    A. choose a plan of action   B. introduce something new
    C. strengthen   D. inspire   E. intend

15. ASPIRATION means *most nearly*

    A. solution
    B. recommendation
    C. preparation
    D. brooding
    E. ambition

16. To IMPLICATE means *most nearly* to

    A. impair   B. agitate   C. involve   D. originate   E. imply

17. SPURIOUS means *most nearly*

    A. false   B. serious   C. inactive   D. strange   E. curious

18. To EMULATE means *most nearly* to

    A. strive to equal   B. arouse to action   C. tear apart
    D. confide in   E. amend

19. STRINGENT means *most nearly*

    A. clear   B. severe   C. loose   D. straight   E. humorous

20. VEHEMENT means *most nearly*

    A. invidious   B. honest   C. calm   D. intense   E. vivid

---

KEYS (CORRECT ANSWERS)

1. B	6. A	11. B	16. C
2. C	7. B	12. C	17. A
3. E	8. D	13. D	18. A
4. D	9. C	14. B	19. B
5. C	10. A	15. E	20. D

TEST 4

DIRECTIONS: For the following questions, select the word or group of words lettered A, B, C, D, or E that means MOST NEARLY the same as the word in capital letters. *PRINT THE LETTER OF THE CORRECT ANSWER IN THE SPACE AT THE RIGHT.*

1. ELATED means *most nearly*
   A. lengthened B. matured C. excited D. youthful E. irate

   1.____

2. SANCTION means *most nearly*
   A. approval B. delay C. priority D. veto E. sanctity

   2.____

3. EGOSTISTIC means *most nearly*
   A. tiresome B. self-centered C. sly
   D. smartly attired E. altruistic

   3.____

4. TRITE means *most nearly*
   A. brilliant B. unusual
   C. funny D. commonplace
   E. tired

   4.____

5. FESTIVE means *most nearly*
   A. edible B. joyous C. proud D. serene E. fatal

   5.____

6. EQUITABLE means *most nearly*
   A. equal B. just C. ordinary D. useful E. similar

   6.____

7. To DISTEND means *most nearly* to
   A. expand B. anger C. crush D. annoy E. distill

   7.____

8. To DERIDE means *most nearly* to
   A. remove B. disdain C. cheer up D. hate E. jeer at

   8.____

9. CRUX means *most nearly*
   A. chief point B. strong action C. criticism
   D. desirable criterion E. weakness

   9.____

10. To AVER means *most nearly* to
    A. consume B. divert C. defy D. assert E. fumble

    10.____

11. APATHY means *most nearly*
    A. sadness B. illness C. hunger D. indifference E. empathy

    11.____

12. PANACEA means *most nearly*
    A. stimulant B. disease C. palace D. diagnosis E. remedy

    12.____

13. ORNATE means *most nearly*

    A. enlightened B. watery C. decorated D. expansive E. onerous

14. UNKEMPT means *most nearly*

    A. untidy
    B. disagreeable
    C. uninformed
    D. crude
    E. illiterate

15. To SATURATE means *most nearly* to

    A. soak B. spoil C. filter D. dye E. dissolve

16. PRECARIOUS means *most nearly*

    A. violent B. uncertain C. troubled D. disastrous E. precious

17. LOQUACIOUS means *most nearly*

    A. grim
    B. talkative
    C. light hearted
    D. hungry
    E. local

18. To JEOPARDIZE means *most nearly* to

    A. offend B. destroy C. discourage D. endanger E. defy

19. BLITHE means *most nearly*

    A. wicked B. merry C. sweet D. pretty E. blind

20. BENEVOLENCE means *most nearly*

    A. good fortune B. well-being C. inheritance
    D. friendship E. charitableness

KEYS (CORRECT ANSWERS)

1. C	6. B	11. D	16. B
2. A	7. A	12. E	17. B
3. B	8. E	13. C	18. D
4. D	9. A	14. A	19. B
5. B	10. D	15. A	20. E

EXAMINATION SECTION
TEST 1

DIRECTIONS: In the space provided at the right, write the letter of the word or expression that most nearly expresses the meaning of the word printed in italics.

1. *Calligraphy*　　　　　　　　　　　　　　　　　　　　　　　　　　　　　　1.____
    - A. weaving
    - B. handwriting
    - C. drafting
    - D. mapmaking

2. *Synchronize*　　　　　　　　　　　　　　　　　　　　　　　　　　　　　　2.____
    - A. happen at the same time
    - B. follow immediately in time
    - C. alternate between events
    - D. postpone to a future time

3. *Semblance*　　　　　　　　　　　　　　　　　　　　　　　　　　　　　　3.____
    - A. surface
    - B. diplomacy
    - C. replacement
    - D. appearance

4. *Circuitous*　　　　　　　　　　　　　　　　　　　　　　　　　　　　　　4.____
    - A. winding
    - B. mutual
    - C. exciting
    - D. rugged

5. *Curtail*　　　　　　　　　　　　　　　　　　　　　　　　　　　　　　　5.____
    - A. threaten
    - B. strengthen
    - C. lessen
    - D. hasten

6. *Noxious*　　　　　　　　　　　　　　　　　　　　　　　　　　　　　　　6.____
    - A. spicy
    - B. smelly
    - C. foreign
    - D. harmful

7. *Drivel*　　　　　　　　　　　　　　　　　　　　　　　　　　　　　　　7.____
    - A. fatigue
    - B. scarcity
    - C. nonsense
    - D. waste

8. *Assuage*　　　　　　　　　　　　　　　　　　　　　　　　　　　　　　　8.____
    - A. soothe
    - B. cleanse
    - C. enjoy
    - D. reward

9. *Intrepid*　　　　　　　　　　　　　　　　　　　　　　　　　　　　　　9.____
    - A. exhausted
    - B. fearless
    - C. anxious
    - D. youthful

10. *Treacherous*　　　　　　　　　　　　　　　　　　　　　　　　　　　　　10.____
    - A. ignorant
    - B. envious
    - C. disloyal
    - D. cowardly

11. The court jester served the role of *buffoon*

    A. horseman B. servant
    C. philosopher D. clown

12. The guest of honor began to speak *nonchalantly* to the audience.

    A. casually B. nervously
    C. seriously D. quietly

13. The governor gave the reporter a *terse* answer to the complex question.

    A. rambling B. inadequate
    C. brief D. ridiculous

14. The servants were told to *adorn* the statues.

    A. decorate B. remove
    C. wash D. destroy

15. Any further discussion of the problem would be *redundant*.

    A. unprofitable B. repetitive
    C. confusing D. misleading

16. The challenge to society is to prevent a criminal from operating with *impunity*.

    A. threats of violence
    B. lack of detection
    C. guarantees of success
    D. freedom from punishment

17. The politician's *candor* surprised his listeners.

    A. honesty B. comments
    C. viewpoint D. examples

18. The horror film was filled with zombies and *cadavers*.

    A. ghosts B. skeletons
    C. monsters D. corpses

19. Leslie worked *diligently* on her school project.

    A. skillfully B. resentfully
    C. industriously D. hurriedly

20. The supervisor could not *coerce* the employee to take early retirement.

    A. request B. force
    C. permit D. advise

21. *Stow*

    A. pack B. report
    C. interest D. beg

22. *Irrepressible*

    A. unrestrainable B. impatient
    C. unknowable D. impractical

23. *Grimace*

    A. important development B. point of view
    C. expression of disgust D. act of spite

24. *Promenade*

    A. limp B. walk
    C. jog D. race

25. *Indicative*

    A. defensive B. attractive
    C. disruptive D. suggestive

26. *Medley*

    A. game B. entertainment
    C. discussion D. mixture

27. *Jaunty*

    A. mighty B. dirty
    C. lively D. petty

28. *Undue*

    A. genuine B. wavy
    C. faultless D. inappropriate

29. *Visage*

    A. appearance B. vividness
    C. prospect D. valor

30. *Avid*

    A. eager B. easy
    C. dry D. flat

31. That *bestial* act marked him for life.

    A. unkind B. insensitive
    C. brutal D. spiteful

32. The professor was regarded as an *erudite* teacher.

    A. rigid B. scholarly
    C. demanding D. reasonable

33. We could see the *knolls* from our window.

    A. rounded hills B. groups of trees
    C. high waves D. marshes

34. As the nurse prepared the shot, I *winced* in anticipation.

    A. moaned aloud B. stared ahead
    C. lay still D. shrank back

35. The president said that he would not *countenance* such policies. 35.____

   A. order
   C. approve
   B. implement
   D. introduce

36. The lawyer proved that the witness was a *prevaricator*. 36.____

   A. murderer
   C. thief
   B. liar
   D. fraud

37. The explorers followed the *tributary* to its origin. 37.____

   A. stream
   C. trail
   B. lake
   D. valley

38. She always comes to school *impeccably* groomed. 38.____

   A. carelessly
   C. stylishly
   B. conservatively
   D. flawlessly

39. Mrs. Royce *discreetly* answered all the questions asked about her neighbor. 39.____

   A. precisely
   C. honestly
   B. tactfully
   D. positively

40. The actor's *feigned* southern accent was praised by the critics. 40.____

   A. pretended
   C. unusual
   B. acquired
   D. low-pitched

KEY (CORRECT ANSWERS)

1. B	11. D	21. A	31. C
2. A	12. A	22. A	32. B
3. D	13. C	23. C	33. A
4. A	14. A	24. B	34. D
5. C	15. B	25. D	35. C
6. D	16. D	26. D	36. B
7. C	17. A	27. C	37. A
8. A	18. D	28. D	38. D
9. B	19. C	29. A	39. B
10. C	20. B	30. A	40. A

TEST 2

DIRECTIONS: In the space provided at the right, write the letter of the word or expression that most nearly expresses the meaning of the word printed in italics.

1. *Abduct*

    A. ruin
    B. aid
    C. fight
    D. kidnap

2. *Demerit*

    A. outcome
    B. fault
    C. prize
    D. notice

3. *Mutinous*

    A. silent
    B. oceangoing
    C. rebellious
    D. miserable

4. *Negligent*

    A. lax
    B. desperate
    C. cowardly
    D. ambitious

5. *Contest*

    A. disturb
    B. dispute
    C. detain
    D. distrust

6. *Query*

    A. wait
    B. lose
    C. show
    D. ask

7. *Insidious*

    A. treacherous
    B. excitable
    C. internal
    D. distracting

8. *Palpitate*

    A. mash
    B. stifle
    C. throb
    D. pace

9. *Animosity*

    A. hatred
    B. interest
    C. silliness
    D. amusement

10. *Egotism*

    A. sociability
    B. aggressiveness
    C. self-confidence
    D. conceit

11. Bob's account of the accident *incriminated* others.

    A. annoyed
    B. involved
    C. ignored
    D. helped

12. When Jack left his position as chief of staff, he was completely *demoralized*.

    A. satisfied
    B. frenzied
    C. liberated
    D. disheartened

13. The architect designed a modern *edifice* of wood and red glass.

    A. framework
    B. platform
    C. structure
    D. false front

14. The speaker kept the meeting interesting with her *facetious* remarks.

    A. amusing
    B. informal
    C. personal
    D. factual

15. The new ruling set a *precedent* for all similar cases that would be tried in court.

    A. direction
    B. standard
    C. regulation
    D. test

16. The botanist wanted a picture of the tree because it was so *gnarled*.

    A. old
    B. unusual
    C. fruitful
    D. deformed

17. Harriet's *ostentatious* display of wealth is upsetting to her friends.

    A. frequent
    B. thoughtless
    C. showy
    D. unnatural

18. The answer was too *oblique* to receive full credit.

    A. indirect
    B. repetitive
    C. disorganized
    D. brief

19. The magician did the sleight-of-hand trick with remarkable *dexterity*.

    A. swiftness
    B. assurance
    C. charisma
    D. skill

20. The principal had no *qualms* about suspending the three boys for fighting.

    A. comments
    B. misgivings
    C. arguments
    D. regrets

21. *Resurrection*

    A. reassurance
    B. encouragement
    C. fascination
    D. revival

22. *Recede*

    A. take over
    B. show off
    C. hold out
    D. move back

23. *Fissure*

    A. opening
    B. path
    C. mountain
    D. landslide

24. *Delectable*

    A. carefree B. elaborate
    C. delightful D. deliberate

25. *Oblivious*

    A. understated B. unmindful
    C. untrue D. unappetizing

26. *Inevitable*

    A. unable B. forceful
    C. certain D. plain

27. *Paradox*

    A. incomplete response B. sharp comment
    C. obvious truth D. seeming contradiction

28. *Cataclysm*

    A. disaster B. deception
    C. denial D. debate

29. *Sanction*

    A. stop B. expel
    C. approve D. refund

30. *Assiduously*

    A. decidedly B. diligently
    C. randomly D. correctly

31. The judge ordered that *restitution* be provided for the robbery victims.

    A. apologies B. recognition
    C. publicity D. compensation

32. The trumpets announced the *imminent* arrival of the dignitary.

    A. approaching B. delayed
    C. unexpected D. distant

33. The shopper was *indignant* at the treatment given him by the clerk.

    A. embarrassed B. pleased
    C. angry D. surprised

34. The cook in the old diner had a *slatternly* appearance.

    A. dreary B. sloppy
    C. homey D. strange

35. The *nebulous* argument that he presented failed to explain the main issue.

    A. careful B. complex
    C. vague D. idealistic

36. The prisoner longed for the life of a *vagabond*. 36.____

    A. wanderer B. millionaire
    C. celebrity D. journalist

37. The entire neighborhood came out to see the *celestial* display. 37.____

    A. artistic B. fantastic
    C. unusual D. heavenly

38. Because the shopkeeper was upset, we were unable to *glean* the details of the robbery. 38.____

    A. connect B. gather
    C. tell D. comprehend

39. The problem rests not with her beliefs but with her excessive desire to *propagate* them. 39.____

    A. spread B. live up to
    C. protect D. justify

40. The young athlete tried to *emulate* his high school coach. 40.____

    A. obey B. assist
    C. imitate D. deceive

KEY (CORRECT ANSWERS)

1.	D	11.	B	21.	D	31.	D
2.	B	12.	D	22.	D	32.	A
3.	C	13.	C	23.	A	33.	C
4.	A	14.	A	24.	C	34.	B
5.	B	15.	B	25.	B	35.	C
6.	D	16.	D	26.	C	36.	A
7.	A	17.	C	27.	D	37.	D
8.	C	18.	A	28.	A	38.	B
9.	A	19.	D	29.	C	39.	A
10.	D	20.	B	30.	B	40.	C

TEST 3

DIRECTIONS: In the space provided at the right, write the letter of the word or expression that most nearly expresses the meaning of the word printed in italics.

1. *Intuition*

    A. payment B. faith
    C. introduction D. insight

2. *Compel*

    A. lengthen B. help
    C. force D. distract

3. *Vent*

    A. discharge B. omit
    C. entertain D. worship

4. *Cohort*

    A. commander B. companion
    C. candidate D. craftsman

5. *Ordeal*

    A. alternate route B. logical sequence
    C. important duty D. severe trial

6. *Fabrication*

    A. addition B. remedy
    C. analysis D. creation

7. *Unwitting*

    A. ordinary B. unaware
    C. unnecessary D. unadvisable

8. *Zealot*

    A. sharp tool B. worthy cause
    C. eager person D. extinct animal

9. *Indulge*

    A. spoil B. surprise
    C. direct D. compare

10. *Hamper*

    A. offer B. confuse
    C. order D. restrict

11. The first settlers in America faced a cold winter in the *vast* wilderness.

    A. unknown B. untamed
    C. enormous D. empty

12. Her very presence at the party *nettled* the other guests. 12.____

    A. embarrassed   B. irritated
    C. puzzled   D. quieted

13. The attorney was eager to *disclose* her evidence. 13.____

    A. examine   B. reorganize
    C. report   D. reveal

14. When the brakes failed, the bus nearly went off the road into a *chasm*. 14.____

    A. gorge   B. field
    C. river   D. wall

15. I avoid that restaurant because of its *insipid* food. 15.____

    A. spicy   B. tasteless
    C. overcooked   D. expensive

16. A *malicious* person is usually unpopular. 16.____

    A. conceited   B. selfish
    C. spiteful   D. stingy

17. He was able to *elude* the soldiers for only a short time. 17.____

    A. escape   B. train
    C. aid   D. restrain

18. The man *denounced* his neighbor because of her political activities. 18.____

    A. avoided   B. ridiculed
    C. spied on   D. condemned

19. The grapegrowers in California employ many *transient* workers. 19.____

    A. immigrant   B. youthful
    C. temporary   D. experienced

20. The money has been *allocated* for new school buses. 20.____

    A. set aside   B. raised
    C. spent   D. borrowed

21. *Larceny* 21.____

    A. criminal   B. burning
    C. name-calling   D. theft

22. *Simulate* 22.____

    A. delay   B. supply
    C. pretend   D. deny

23. *Lucid* 23.____

    A. clear   B. colorful
    C. lawful   D. old

24. *Remorse*

    A. anger
    B. regret
    C. apology
    D. coldness

    24.____

25. *Laden*

    A. optimistic
    B. refined
    C. burdened
    D. worried

    25.____

26. *Turbulence*

    A. control
    B. interruption
    C. renewal
    D. disorder

    26.____

27. *Incessantly*

    A. instantly
    B. brilliantly
    C. respectfully
    D. continually

    27.____

28. *Chronic*

    A. diseased
    B. constant
    C. aged
    D. unsafe

    28.____

29. *Tepid*

    A. lukewarm
    B. eager
    C. tearful
    D. sharp

    29.____

30. *Consensus*

    A. survey
    B. contract
    C. association
    D. agreement

    30.____

31. Have you ever heard the saying, "To be *wary* is to be wise"?

    A. Thrifty
    B. Healthy
    C. Careful
    D. Industrious

    31.____

32. Sherlock Holmes was noted for his superb power of *deduction*.

    A. imagination
    B. reasoning
    C. extrasensory perception
    D. concentration

    32.____

33. The manager encouraged the staff to try to add to the store's *clientele*.

    A. good will
    B. profits
    C. customers
    D. variety of merchandise

    33.____

34. The student was *disconcerted* when she saw her test score.

    A. upset
    B. assured
    C. pleased
    D. surprised

    34.____

35. An automobile can be a *lethal* machine.

    A. expensive
    B. deadly
    C. essential
    D. magnificent

    35.____

36. The general promised to *annihilate* the enemy's troops. 36._____

    A. pursue
    B. destroy
    C. capture
    D. surround

37. She is the owner of a *lucrative* construction company. 37._____

    A. small
    B. reliable
    C. local
    D. profitable

38. After Joan had completed her investigation, she realized that her *premise* was incorrect. 38._____

    A. assumption
    B. conclusion
    C. methodology
    D. information

39. During the campaign, the politicians often engaged in *acrimonious* debate. 39._____

    A. meaningless
    B. brilliant
    C. bitter
    D. loud

40. There is no value in this *sordid* film. 40._____

    A. boring
    B. vile
    C. experimental
    D. inferior

KEY (CORRECT ANSWERS)

1.	D	11.	C	21.	D	31.	C
2.	C	12.	B	22.	C	32.	B
3.	A	13.	D	23.	A	33.	C
4.	B	14.	A	24.	B	34.	A
5.	D	15.	B	25.	C	35.	B
6.	D	16.	C	26.	D	36.	B
7.	B	17.	A	27.	D	37.	D
8.	C	18.	D	28.	B	38.	A
9.	A	19.	C	29.	A	39.	C
10.	D	20.	A	30.	D	40.	B

TEST 4

DIRECTIONS: In the space provided at the right, write the letter of the word or expression that most nearly expresses the meaning of the word printed in italics.

1. *Defame* 1.____

    A. slander B. depress
    C. outwit D. arouse

2. *Retaliation* 2.____

    A. recommendation B. list
    C. revenge D. victory

3. *Zeal* 3.____

    A. boredom B. enthusiasm
    C. compassion D. trust

4. *Unilateral* 4.____

    A. one-wheeled B. unanticipated
    C. similar D. one-sided

5. *Gratuity* 5.____

    A. tip for service B. tool for printing
    C. medal for achievement D. thank you note

6. *Bewitch* 6.____

    A. repel B. fascinate
    C. satisfy D. fear

7. *Desist* 7.____

    A. cause B. change
    C. help D. stop

8. *Bigotry* 8.____

    A. invention B. obstruction
    C. intolerance D. belief

9. *Somber* 9.____

    A. gloomy B. gentle
    C. lively D. careful

10. *Redemption* 10.____

    A. power B. sale
    C. religion D. deliverance

11. The *eccentric* old lady loved her cats, her hats, and her tumble-down house. 11.____

    A. moody B. lovable
    C. strange D. friendly

81

12. The author was totally displeased with the *abridged* version of his novel.

    A. televised
    B. shortened
    C. translated
    D. censored

13. He made the statement *assertively*.

    A. reluctantly
    B. hastily
    C. positively
    D. honestly

14. Because of his *inertia,* he seldom achieves his goal.

    A. temper
    B. laziness
    C. stupidity
    D. carelessness

15. The executive believes that people must be *ruthless* in order to succeed in business.

    A. powerful
    B. dishonest
    C. reckless
    D. merciless

16. The actress was described as having *mediocre* talent.

    A. ordinary
    B. uncommon
    C. excellent
    D. inferior

17. The *gaudy* dress is trimmed with pearls.

    A. elegant
    B. worn out
    C. pretty
    D. flashy

18. The class *extolled* the virtues of their teacher.

    A. listed
    B. praised
    C. apologized for
    D. explained

19. The child was both *gregarious* and hardworking in school.

    A. comfortable
    B. prompt
    C. sociable
    D. happy

20. Many *credulous* people are influenced by television advertisements to buy certain products.

    A. believing
    B. uneducated
    C. clever
    D. logical

21. *Tantalize*

    A. encourage
    B. tease
    C. satisfy
    D. quarrel

22. *Proximity*

    A. falseness
    B. correctness
    C. favor
    D. nearness

23. *Perceptible*

    A. capable
    B. likeable
    C. observable
    D. returnable

24. *Philanthropy*

    A. love of money
    B. love of humanity
    C. love of stamps
    D. love of words

25. *Havoc*

    A. respect
    B. danger
    C. destruction
    D. complications

26. *Consolidate*

    A. unite
    B. sympathize
    C. void
    D. profit

27. *Discrepancy*

    A. reduction
    B. restraint
    C. looseness
    D. difference

28. *Advocate* (verb)

    A. recommend
    B. supply
    C. remove
    D. vote

29. *Sedate*

    A. seated
    B. composed
    C. bored
    D. informal

30. *Superficial*

    A. buried
    B. overhead
    C. external
    D. important

31. Canoeing through the rapids is a *grueling* experience.

    A. exciting
    B. uncomfortable
    C. rewarding
    D. exhausting

32. He was *cognizant* of his responsibilities.

    A. aware
    B. afraid
    C. weary
    D. relieved

33. With Joe's *tenacity*, he is bound to succeed.

    A. intelligence
    B. luck
    C. talent
    D. persistence

34. When will the sales campaign be *initiated*?

    A. Approved
    B. Planned
    C. Started
    D. Tested

35. Joan's *vitality* is envied by many people.

    A. beauty
    B. energy
    C. ability
    D. popularity

36. In view of the circumstances, Jane's comment seemed *callous*.

    A. insensitive
    B. misleading
    C. kind
    D. true

37. Reading the letter left him in a *pensive* mood.

    A. calm
    B. thoughtful
    C. happy
    D. romantic

38. He answered the question *impetuously*.

    A. foolishly
    B. hastily
    C. quietly
    D. honestly

39. His *inane* suggestion fell on deaf ears.

    A. silly
    B. detailed
    C. unusual
    D. selfish

40. After being lost in the woods, Tom was *ravenous*.

    A. extremely tired
    B. extremely thirsty
    C. extremely hungry
    D. extremely angry

KEY (CORRECT ANSWERS)

1.	A	11.	C	21.	B	31.	D
2.	C	12.	B	22.	D	32.	A
3.	B	13.	C	23.	C	33.	D
4.	D	14.	B	24.	B	34.	C
5.	A	15.	D	25.	C	35.	B
6.	B	16.	A	26.	A	36.	A
7.	D	17.	D	27.	D	37.	B
8.	C	18.	B	28.	A	38.	B
9.	A	19.	C	29.	B	39.	A
10.	D	20.	A	30.	C	40.	C

WORD MEANING

EXAMINATION SECTION
TEST 1

DIRECTIONS: Each question or incomplete statement is followed by several suggested answers or completions. Select the one that BEST answers the question or completes the statement. *PRINT THE LETTER OF THE CORRECT ANSWER IN THE SPACE AT THE RIGHT.*

1. Local responsibility for the relief of economic need long having been recognized as inadequate, the state and federal governments have established schemes of *categorical* assistance and social insurance.
   In the preceding sentence, the italicized word means MOST NEARLY

   A. conditional B. economic
   C. pecuniary   D. classified

   1._____

2. When a person *vicariously* lives out his own problems in novels and plays, he is engaging in an experience that is, in terms of the italicized word in this sentence,

   A. dynamic   B. monastic
   C. substituted D. dignified

   2._____

3. The Alcoholics Anonymous program, which in essence amounts to a *therapeutic* procedure, is codified into twelve steps. The italicized word in the preceding sentence means MOST NEARLY

   A. compensatory B. curative
   C. sequential   D. volitional

   3._____

4. The professor developed a different central theme during every *semester*.
   The italicized word in the preceding sentence means MOST NEARLY

   A. bi-annual period of instruction
   B. orientation period
   C. slide demonstration
   D. weekly lecture series

   4._____

5. To say that the Community Chest movement seems to have been *indigenous* to the North American continent describes this movement, in terms of the italicized word in this sentence, MOST NEARLY as

   A. imported   B. essential
   C. native   D. homogeneous

   5._____

6. There should be no *opprobrium* attached to the term "second-hand housing" since every house is second-hand after the first occupancy.
   The italicized word in the preceding sentence means MOST NEARLY

   A. stigma   B. honor   C. rank   D. credit

   6._____

85

7. Clinics are now seeing many people who complain of seriously disturbed feelings and other symptoms relating to *traumatic* war experiences.
   In the preceding sentence, the italicized word means MOST NEARLY

   A. recent
   B. worldwide
   C. prodigious
   D. shocking

8. The nature of the *pathology* underlying the compulsion is obscure.
   In the preceding sentence, the italicized word means MOST NEARLY

   A. drive
   B. disease
   C. deterioration
   D. development

9. If the interests of a social welfare agency are concerned with bringing opportunities for self-help to underprivileged *ethnic* groups, its activities involve MOST NEARLY, in terms of the italicized word in this sentence,

   A. racial factors
   B. minority units
   C. religious affiliations
   D. economic conditions

10. Increased facilities for medical care (though interrupted to some extent by the *exigencies* of wartime) will safeguard the health of many children who in previous generations would have been doomed to an early death or to physical disability.
    In the preceding sentence, the MOST NEARLY CORRECT equivalent of the italicized word is

    A. obstacles
    B. occurrences
    C. extenuations
    D. exactions

11. He described a hypothetical situation to illustrate his point.
    In the preceding sentence, the word *hypothetical* means MOST NEARLY

    A. actual
    B. theoretical
    C. typical
    D. unusual

12. I gave tacit approval to my partner's proposed business changes.
    In the preceding sentence, the word *tacit* means MOST NEARLY

    A. enthusiastic
    B. partial
    C. silent
    D. written

13. Jones was considered an astute lawyer by the members of his profession.
    In the preceding sentence, the word *astute* means MOST NEARLY

    A. clever
    B. persevering
    C. poorly trained
    D. unethical

14. There were intimations even in early days of the way in which he would go.
    In the preceding sentence, the word *intimations* means MOST NEARLY

    A. hints
    B. patterns
    C. plans
    D. purposes

15. His last book was published posthumously.
    In the preceding sentence, the word *posthumously* means MOST NEARLY

    A. after the death of the author
    B. printed free by the publisher
    C. without a dedication
    D. without royalties

16. When he was challenged, he used every known subterfuge. In the preceding sentence, the word *subterfuge* means MOST NEARLY

    A. evasion to justify one's conduct
    B. means of attack to defend one's self
    C. medical device
    D. unconscious thought

17. His partner suggested a course of action that would alleviate the difficulties which confronted him.
    In the preceding sentence, the word *alleviate* means MOST NEARLY

    A. correct   B. lessen   C. remove   D. solve

18. Among the applicants for the new apartment, white collar workers were preponderant.
    In the preceding sentence, the word *preponderant* means MOST NEARLY

    A. considered not eligible   B. in evidence
    C. superior in number   D. the first to apply

19. The captain gave a lucid explanation of his plans for the coming campaign.
    In the preceding sentence, the word *lucid* means MOST NEARLY

    A. clear   B. graphic
    C. interesting   D. thorough

20. He led a sedentary life.
    In the preceding sentence, the word *sedentary* means MOST NEARLY

    A. aimless   B. exciting   C. full   D. inactive

21. His plan for the next campaign was very plausible.
    In the preceding sentence, the word *plausible* means MOST NEARLY

    A. appropriate   B. believable
    C. usable   D. valuable

22. The office manager thought it advisable to mollify his subordinate.
    The word *mollify*, as used in this sentence, means MOST NEARLY

    A. reprimand   B. caution   C. calm   D. question

23. The bureau chief adopted a dilatory policy.
    The word *dilatory*, as used in this sentence, means MOST NEARLY

    A. tending to cause delay
    B. acceptable to all affected
    C. severe but fair
    D. prepared with great care

24. He complained about the paucity of requests.
    The word *paucity*, as used in this sentence, means MOST NEARLY

    A. great variety   B. unreasonableness
    C. unexpected increase   D. scarcity

25. To say that an event is *imminent* means MOST NEARLY that it is

    A. near at hand
    B. unpredictable
    C. favorable or happy
    D. very significant

26. The general manager delivered a laudatory speech.
    The word *laudatory,* as used in this sentence, means MOST NEARLY

    A. clear and emphatic
    B. lengthy
    C. introductory
    D. expressing praise

27. We all knew of his aversion for performing statistical work.
    The word *aversion,* as used in this sentence, means MOST NEARLY

    A. training
    B. dislike
    C. incentive
    D. lack of preparation

28. The engineer was circumspect in making his recommendations.
    The word *circumspect,* as used in this sentence, means MOST NEARLY

    A. hostile   B. outspoken   C. biased   D. cautious

29. To say that certain clerical operations were *obviated* means MOST NEARLY that these operations were

    A. extremely distasteful
    B. easily understood
    C. made unnecessary
    D. very complicated

30. The interviewer was impressed with the client's demeanor. The word *demeanor,* as used in this sentence, means MOST NEARLY

    A. outward manner
    B. plan of action
    C. fluent speech
    D. extensive knowledge

31. To say that the information was *gratuitous* means MOST NEARLY that it was

    A. given freely
    B. deeply appreciated
    C. brief
    D. valuable

32. She considered the supervisor's action to be arbitrary. The word *arbitrary,* as used in this sentence, means MOST NEARLY

    A. inconsistent
    B. justifiable
    C. appeasing
    D. dictatorial

33. He sent the irate employee to the personnel manager. The word *irate* means MOST NEARLY

    A. irresponsible
    B. untidy
    C. insubordinate
    D. angry

34. An *ambiguous* statement is one which is

    A. forceful and convincing
    B. capable of being understood in more than one sense
    C. based upon good judgment and sound reasoning processes
    D. uninteresting and too lengthy

35. To *extol* means MOST NEARLY to

   A. summon   B. praise   C. reject   D. withdraw

36. The word *proximity* means MOST NEARLY

   A. similarity
   B. exactness
   C. harmony
   D. nearness

37. His friends had a detrimental influence on him.
   The word *detrimental* means MOST NEARLY

   A. favorable
   B. lasting
   C. harmful
   D. short-lived

38. The chief inspector relied upon the veracity of his inspectors.
   The word *veracity* means MOST NEARLY

   A. speed
   B. assistance
   C. shrewdness
   D. truthfulness

39. There was much diversity in the suggestions submitted.
   The word *diversity* means MOST NEARLY

   A. similarity
   B. value
   C. triviality
   D. variety

40. The survey was concerned with the problem of indigence.
   The word *indigence* means MOST NEARLY

   A. poverty
   B. corruption
   C. intolerance
   D. morale

41. The investigator considered this evidence to be extraneous.
   The word *extraneous* means MOST NEARLY

   A. significant
   B. pertinent but unobtainable
   C. not essential
   D. inadequate

42. He was surprised at the temerity of the new employee.
   The word *temerity* means MOST NEARLY

   A. shyness
   B. enthusiasm
   C. rashness
   D. self-control

43. The term *ex officio* means MOST NEARLY

   A. expelled from office
   B. a former holder of a high office
   C. without official approval
   D. by virtue of office or position

44. The aims of the students and the aims of the faculty often coincide.
   The word *coincide* means MOST NEARLY

   A. agree
   B. are ignored
   C. conflict
   D. are misinterpreted

45. The secretary of the department was responsible for setting up an index of relevant magazine articles.
The word *relevant* means MOST NEARLY

    A. applicable
    B. controversial
    C. miscellaneous
    D. recent

46. One of the secretary's duties consisted of sorting and filing facsimiles of student term papers.
The word *facsimiles* means MOST NEARLY

    A. bibliographical listings
    B. exact copies
    C. summaries
    D. supporting documentation

47. Stringent requirements for advanced physics courses often result in small class sizes.
The word *stringent* means MOST NEARLY

    A. lengthy
    B. remarkable
    C. rigid
    D. vague

48. The professor explained that the report was too verbose to be submitted.
The word *verbose* means MOST NEARLY

    A. brief   B. specific   C. general   D. wordy

49. The faculty meeting pre-empted the conference room in the Dean's office.
The word *pre-empted* means MOST NEARLY

    A. appropriated
    B. emptied
    C. filled
    D. reserved

50. The professor's credentials became a subject of controversy.
The word *controversy* means MOST NEARLY

    A. annoyance   B. debate   C. envy   D. review

KEY (CORRECT ANSWERS)

1. D	11. B	21. B	31. A	41. C
2. C	12. C	22. C	32. D	42. C
3. B	13. A	23. A	33. D	43. D
4. A	14. A	24. D	34. B	44. A
5. C	15. A	25. A	35. B	45. A
6. A	16. A	26. D	36. D	46. B
7. D	17. B	27. B	37. C	47. C
8. B	18. C	28. D	38. D	48. D
9. A	19. A	29. C	39. D	49. A
10. D	20. D	30. A	40. A	50. B

TEST 2

DIRECTIONS: Each question or incomplete statement is followed by several suggested answers or completions. Select the one that BEST answers the question or completes the statement. *PRINT THE LETTER OF THE CORRECT ANSWER IN THE SPACE AT THE RIGHT.*

1. The suspect was detained until a witness proved he could not have committed the crime.
   As used in this sentence, the word *detained* means MOST NEARLY

   A. suspected   B. accused   C. held   D. observed

2. The fireman's equilibrium improved shortly after he had stumbled out of the smoke-filled building.
   As used in this sentence, the word *equilibrium* means MOST NEARLY

   A. breathing   B. balance   C. vision   D. vigor

3. The water supply in the tank began to dwindle soon after the pumps were turned on.
   As used in this sentence, the word *dwindle* means MOST NEARLY

   A. grow smaller
   B. whirl about
   C. become muddy
   D. overflow

4. They thought his illness was feigned.
   As used in this sentence, the word *feigned* means MOST NEARLY

   A. hereditary
   B. contagious
   C. pretended
   D. incurable

5. The officer corroborated the information given by the fireman.
   As used in this sentence, the word *corroborated* means MOST NEARLY

   A. questioned
   B. confirmed
   C. corrected
   D. accepted

6. Only after an inspection were they even able to surmise what caused the fire.
   As used in this sentence, the word *surmise* means MOST NEARLY

   A. guess   B. discover   C. prove   D. isolate

7. Officers shall report all flagrant violations of regulations or laws by subordinates.
   As used in this sentence, the word *flagrant* means MOST NEARLY

   A. glaring
   B. accidental
   C. habitual
   D. minor

8. The man was cajoled into signing the contract.
   As used in this sentence, the word *cajoled* means MOST NEARLY

   A. bribed   B. coaxed   C. confused   D. forced

9. The announcement was met with general derision.
   As used in this sentence, the word *derision* means MOST NEARLY

   A. anger   B. applause   C. disbelief   D. ridicule

10. The speaker's words were moving but irrelevant.
    As used in this sentence, the word *irrelevant* means MOST NEARLY

    A. insincere
    B. not based upon facts
    C. not bearing upon the subject under discussion
    D. self-contradictory

11. The breakdown of the machine was due to a defective gasket.
    As used in this sentence, the word *gasket* means MOST NEARLY

    A. filter   B. piston
    C. sealer   D. transmission

12. The noise of the pneumatic drill disturbed the teacher.
    As used in this sentence, the word *pneumatic* means MOST NEARLY

    A. air pressure   B. electricity
    C. internal combustion D. water pressure

13. He exercised the prerogatives of his office with moderation.
    As used in this sentence, the word *prerogatives* means MOST NEARLY

    A. burdens   B. duties
    C. opportunities   D. privileges

14. He made his decisions after a cursory examination of the facts.
    As used in this sentence, the word *cursory* means MOST NEARLY

    A. biased   B. critical
    C. exhaustive   D. hasty

15. John was appointed provisional chairman of the arrange-ments committee.
    As used in this sentence, the word *provisional* means MOST NEARLY

    A. official   B. permanent
    C. temporary   D. unofficial

16. After the bush is planted, the ground around it should be tamped.
    As used in this sentence, the word *tamped* means MOST NEARLY

    A. loosened   B. packed   C. raked   D. watered

17. The volcano was dormant during the time I visited the island.
    As used in this sentence, the word *dormant* means MOST NEARLY

    A. erupting   B. extinct
    C. inactive   D. threatening

18. A starter's gun is not considered to be a lethal weapon.
    As used in this sentence, the word *lethal* means MOST NEARLY

    A. criminal   B. deadly   C. offensive   D. reliable

19. At the crucial moment, the seismograph failed to function. As used in this sentence, the word *seismograph* means MOST NEARLY an instrument for measuring

    A. earthquakes   B. heartbeats
    C. humidity   D. nuclear radiation

20. The supervisor's instructions were terse.
    As used in this sentence, the word *terse* means MOST NEARLY

    A. detailed   B. harsh   C. vague   D. concise

21. He did not wish to evade these issues.
    As used in this sentence, the word *evade* means MOST NEARLY

    A. avoid   B. examine   C. settle   D. discuss

22. The prospects for an early settlement were dubious.
    As used in this sentence, the word *dubious* means MOST NEARLY

    A. strengthened   B. uncertain
    C. weakened   D. cheerful

23. The visitor was morose.
    As used in this sentence, the word *morose* means MOST NEARLY

    A. curious   B. gloomy   C. impatient   D. timid

24. He was unwilling to impede the work of his unit.
    As used in this sentence, the word *impede* means MOST NEARLY

    A. carry out   B. criticize   C. praise   D. hinder

25. The remuneration was unsatisfactory.
    As used in this sentence, the word *remuneration* means MOST NEARLY

    A. payment   B. summary
    C. explanation   D. estimate

26. A *recurring* problem is one that

    A. replaces a problem that existed previously
    B. is unexpected
    C. has long been overlooked
    D. comes up from time to time

27. His subordinates were aware of this magnanimous act. As used in this sentence, the word *magnanimous* means MOST NEARLY

    A. insolent   B. shrewd
    C. unselfish   D. threatening

28. The new employee is a zealous worker.
    As used in this sentence, the word *zealous* means MOST NEARLY

    A. awkward   B. untrustworthy
    C. enthusiastic   D. skillful

29. To *impair* means MOST NEARLY to

    A. weaken   B. conceal   C. improve   D. expose

30. The unit head was in a quandary.
    As used in this sentence, the word *quandary* means MOST NEARLY

    A. violent dispute   B. puzzling predicament
    C. angry mood   D. strong position

31. His actions were judicious.
    As used in this sentence, the word *judicious* means MOST NEARLY

    A. wise   B. biased   C. final   D. limited

32. His report contained many irrelevant statements.
    As used in this sentence, the word *irrelevant* means MOST NEARLY

    A. unproven   B. not pertinent
    C. hard to understand D. insincere

33. He was not present at the inception of the program.
    As used in this sentence, the word *inception* means MOST NEARLY

    A. beginning   B. discussion
    C. conclusion   D. rejection

34. The word *solicitude* means MOST NEARLY

    A. request   B. isolation
    C. seriousness D. concern

35. He was asked to pacify the visitor.
    As used in this sentence, the word *pacify* means MOST NEARLY

    A. escort   B. interview   C. calm   D. detain

36. To say that a certain document is *authentic* means MOST NEARLY that it is

    A. fictitious   B. well written
    C. priceless   D. genuine

37. A clerk who is *meticulous* in performing his work is one who is

    A. alert to improved techniques
    B. likely to be erratic and unpredictable
    C. excessively careful of small details
    D. slovenly and inaccurate

38. A pamphlet which is *replete* with charts and graphs is one which

    A. deals with the construction of charts and graphs
    B. is full of charts and graphs
    C. substitutes illustrations for tabulated data
    D. is in need of charts and graphs

39. His former secretary was diligent in carrying out her duties.
    The word *diligent* means MOST NEARLY

    A. incompetent   B. cheerful
    C. careless   D. industrious

40. To *supersede* means MOST NEARLY to

    A. take the place of   B. come before
    C. be in charge of   D. divide into equal parts

41. A person is a *tyro* if he is MOST NEARLY a

    A. charlatan   B. novice
    C. scholar   D. talebearer

42. A tenant who is *adamant* in his complaints about the noise emanating from the neighboring apartment is MOST NEARLY

    A. belligerent   B. justified
    C. petty   D. unyielding

43. The assistant, according to his supervisor's report, had performed his tasks assiduously. The word *assiduously* means MOST NEARLY

    A. diligently   B. expertly
    C. inefficiently   D. reluctantly

44. The current exigency of affairs at the Authority was given as the reason for the decision. The word *exigency* means MOST NEARLY

    A. conduct   B. investigation
    C. trend   D. urgency

45. The discovery of the defalcation was made by the manager. The word *defalcation* means MOST NEARLY

    A. damage   B. error   C. fraud   D. theft

46. The halcyon days that followed could not have been predicted. The word *halcyon* means MOST NEARLY

    A. eventful   B. festive
    C. frenzied   D. untroubled

47. The assistant submitted a sententious report after he had made his investigation. The word *sententious* means MOST NEARLY

    A. laudatory   B. pithy
    C. tentative   D. unfavorable

48. An assistant should be characterized as *saturnine* if he is MOST NEARLY

    A. apathetic   B. enigmatic   C. gloomy   D. sarcastic

49. A situation arising at a project is *anomalous* if the situation is MOST NEARLY

    A. irritating   B. perplexing
    C. recurrent   D. unusual

50. The Housing Authority did what it could to palliate the condition about which the tenants had complained. The word *palliate* means MOST NEARLY

    A. reconsider   B. rectify
    C. relieve   D. remedy

KEY (CORRECT ANSWERS)

1. C	11. C	21. A	31. A	41. B
2. B	12. A	22. B	32. B	42. D
3. A	13. D	23. B	33. A	43. A
4. C	14. D	24. D	34. D	44. D
5. B	15. C	25. A	35. C	45. D
6. A	16. B	26. D	36. D	46. D
7. A	17. C	27. C	37. C	47. B
8. B	18. B	28. C	38. B	48. C
9. D	19. A	29. A	39. D	49. D
10. C	20. D	30. B	40. A	50. C

TEST 3

DIRECTIONS: Each question or incomplete statement is followed by several suggested answers or completions. Select the one that BEST answers the question or completes the statement. *PRINT THE LETTER OF THE CORRECT ANSWER IN THE SPACE AT THE RIGHT.*

1. The employees were skeptical about the usefulness of the new procedure.
   The word *skeptical,* as used in this sentence, means MOST NEARLY

   A. enthusiastic
   B. indifferent
   C. doubtful
   D. misinformed

   1.____

2. He presented abstruse reasons in defense of his proposal.
   The word *abstruse,* as used in this sentence, means MOST NEARLY

   A. unnecessary under the circumstances
   B. apparently without merit or value
   C. hard to be understood
   D. obviously sound

   2.____

3. A program of austerity is in effect in many countries. The word *austerity,* as used in this sentence, means MOST NEARLY

   A. rigorous self-restraint
   B. military censorship
   C. rugged individualism
   D. self-indulgence

   3.____

4. The terms of the contract were abrogated at the last meeting of the board.
   The word *abrogated,* as used in this sentence, means MOST NEARLY

   A. discussed
   B. summarized
   C. agreed upon
   D. annulled

   4.____

5. The enforcement of stringent regulations is a difficult task.
   The word *stringent,* as used in this sentence, means MOST NEARLY

   A. unreasonable
   B. strict
   C. unpopular
   D. obscure

   5.____

6. You should not disparage the value of his suggestions. The word *disparage,* as used in this sentence, means MOST NEARLY

   A. ignore
   B. exaggerate
   C. belittle
   D. reveal

   6.____

7. The employee's conduct was considered reprehensible by his superior.
   The word *reprehensible,* as used in this sentence, means MOST NEARLY

   A. worthy of reward or honor
   B. in accordance with rules and regulations
   C. detrimental to efficiency and morale
   D. deserving of censure or rebuke

   7.____

8. He said he would emulate the persistence of his co-workers. The word *emulate,* as used in this sentence, means MOST NEARLY

   A. strive to equal
   B. acknowledge
   C. encourage
   D. attach no significance to

   8.____

9. The revised regulations on discipline contained several mitigating provisions.
   The word *mitigating,* as used in this sentence, means MOST NEARLY

   A. making more effective
   B. containing contradictions
   C. rendering less harsh
   D. producing much criticism

10. The arrival of the inspector at the office on that day was fortuitous.
    The word *fortuitous,* as used in this sentence, means MOST NEARLY

    A. accidental
    B. unfortunate
    C. prearranged
    D. desirable

11. The development of the program received its real impetus in the recent action of the commissioner.
    The word *impetus,* as used in this sentence, means MOST NEARLY

    A. formulation
    B. impediment
    C. implementation
    D. stimulus

12. However, the purpose is not to be pedantic but to be practical.
    The word *pedantic,* as used in this sentence, means MOST NEARLY

    A. affected
    B. philosophical
    C. progressive
    D. scientific

13. There is much just criticism of the dilatoriness with which many large organizations perform their work and the red tape that is required in the discharge of official duties.
    The word *dilatoriness,* as used in this sentence, means MOST NEARLY

    A. complications
    B. delay
    C. dilations
    D. splendor

14. If it appears that this report moves occasionally into the general field of administrative problems, your indulgence is asked, since it seems to us that voices should be heard wherever possible in behalf of sound, scientific public administration.
    The word *indulgence,* as used in this sentence, means MOST NEARLY

    A. criticism
    B. assistance
    C. forbearance
    D. concentration

15. The supervisor's chief functions as leader are to develop the individuals under him and to integrate them into a cooperative team.
    The word *integrate,* as used in this sentence, means MOST NEARLY

    A. develop   B. mold   C. unify   D. work

16. The impression is widespread that it is inherently impossible to secure the same efficiency and economy in the administration of public affairs that can be secured in the conduct of private undertakings.
    The word *inherently,* as used in this sentence, means MOST NEARLY

    A. admittedly
    B. internally
    C. naturally
    D. practically

17. The production manager had followed an opportunistic policy and had met new requirements as they appeared.
    The word *opportunistic,* as used in this sentence, means MOST NEARLY

    A. efficient
    B. expedient
    C. farsighted
    D. important

18. Therein is epitomized the agricultural revolution which, hand in hand with the industrial revolution, is rebuilding the country and our social life.
    The word *epitomized,* as used in this sentence, means MOST NEARLY

    A. annotated
    B. described
    C. expatriated
    D. summarized

19. A periodic appraisal of the method of effectuating decisions is important.
    The word *effectuating,* as used in this sentence, means MOST NEARLY

    A. affecting
    B. developing
    C. fulfilling
    D. making

20. The classifications of filing material in this office are, then, artificial and overlapping, and are designed for transient convenience.
    The word *transient,* as used in this sentence, means MOST NEARLY

    A. basic
    B. local
    C. operating
    D. temporary

21. From a research standpoint, there is hardly a paucity of material for us to consider.
    The word *paucity*, as used in this sentence, means MOST NEARLY

    A. abundance
    B. adequate amount
    C. insufficiency
    D. unsatisfactory quality

22. This assignment was handled expeditiously.
    The word *expeditiously* means MOST NEARLY

    A. clumsily
    B. without preparation
    C. speedily
    D. on a trial basis

23. Miss Lind is scrupulous in performing her duties.
    The word *scrupulous* means MOST NEARLY

    A. slow
    B. conscientious
    C. careless
    D. gracious

24. To *apprise* means MOST NEARLY to

    A. award
    B. inform
    C. dispossess
    D. discover

25. His report on this matter is opportune.
    The word *opportune* means MOST NEARLY

    A. timely
    B. biased
    C. hostile
    D. hopeful

26. His actions had a deleterious effect on the other employees.
    The word *deleterious* means MOST NEARLY

    A. restraining
    B. highly pleasing
    C. harmful
    D. misleading

27. The size of the staff was increased, and the gain in output was commensurate.
    The word *commensurate* means MOST NEARLY

    A. praiseworthy
    B. enormous
    C. of equal extent
    D. trivial in proportion

28. Miss Hunter is assiduous in keeping these records.
    The word *assiduous* means MOST NEARLY

    A. negligent
    B. untrained
    C. unrestricted
    D. diligent

29. His bookkeeper said that our account was dormant.
    The word *dormant* means MOST NEARLY

    A. inadequate
    B. transferred
    C. inactive
    D. overdrawn

30. The supervisor's criticisms were caustic.
    The word *caustic* means MOST NEARLY

    A. sarcastic and severe
    B. unfair and undeserved
    C. ominous but justified
    D. fitful and unsteady

31. The word *impediment* means MOST NEARLY

    A. hindrance
    B. trick or deception
    C. insinuation
    D. urgent matter

32. This procedure did not preclude errors in judgment.
    The word *preclude* means MOST NEARLY

    A. arise from
    B. prevent
    C. account for
    D. define

33. The statements made at the initial conference were retracted at a subsequent meeting.
    The word *retracted* means MOST NEARLY

    A. developed
    B. criticized
    C. endorsed
    D. withdrawn

34. He was unwilling to supplant his immediate superior.
    The word *supplant* means MOST NEARLY

    A. fill the needs of
    B. request aid from
    C. take the place of
    D. withhold support for

35. Miss Olin has a prepossessing manner.
    The word *prepossessing* means MOST NEARLY

    A. authoritative
    B. likable
    C. apologetic
    D. deceiving

36. The methods used to solve these critical problems were analogous.
    The word *analogous* means MOST NEARLY

    A. similar
    B. unconventional
    C. clever
    D. unsound

37. This letter appears to have been written by some indigent person.
    The word *indigent,* as used in this sentence, means MOST NEARLY

    A. foreign-born
    B. needy
    C. uneducated
    D. angry

38. The conference began under auspicious circumstances.
    The word *auspicious,* as used in this sentence, means MOST NEARLY

    A. favorable
    B. chaotic
    C. questionable
    D. threatening

39. An inordinate amount of work was assigned to the newly appointed clerk.
    The word *inordinate,* as used in this sentence, means MOST NEARLY

    A. unanticipated
    B. adequate
    C. inexcusable
    D. excessive

40. The report which was obtained surreptitiously was very detailed and fully documented.
    The word *surreptitiously,* as used in this sentence, means MOST NEARLY

    A. stealthily
    B. a short time ago
    C. with great difficulty
    D. unexpectedly

41. We all knew him to be a man of probity.
    The word *probity,* as used in this sentence, means MOST NEARLY

    A. culture
    B. proven ability
    C. integrity
    D. dignity and poise

42. He made a cursory study of the problem before starting on the assignment.
    The word *cursory,* as used in this sentence, means MOST NEARLY

    A. detailed
    B. secret
    C. hasty
    D. methodical

43. The regulation had a salutary effect upon the members of the staff.
    The word *salutary,* as used in this sentence, means MOST NEARLY

    A. disturbing
    B. beneficial
    C. confusing
    D. premature

44. The solicitous supervisor discussed the employee's grievances with them.
    The word *solicitous,* as used in this sentence, means MOST NEARLY

    A. concerned
    B. impartial
    C. wise
    D. experienced

45. The employee categorically denied all responsibility for the error.
    The word *categorically,* as used in this sentence, means MOST NEARLY

    A. repeatedly
    B. loudly
    C. hesitantly
    D. absolutely

46. No stipend was specified in the agreement. 46.____
    The word *stipend,* as used in this sentence, means MOST NEARLY

    A. statement of working conditions
    B. receipt for payment
    C. compensation for services
    D. delivery date

47. The supervisor pointed out that the focus of the study was not clear. 47.____
    The word *focus,* as used in this sentence, means MOST NEARLY

    A. end   B. objective   C. follow-up   D. location

48. The faculty of the department agreed that the departmental program was deficient. 48.____
    The word *deficient,* as used in this sentence, means MOST NEARLY

    A. excellent   B. inadequate
    C. demanding   D. sufficient

49. The secretary was asked to type a rough draft of a college course syllabus. 49.____
    The word *syllabus,* as used in this sentence, means MOST NEARLY

    A. directory of departments and services
    B. examination schedule
    C. outline of a course of study
    D. rules and regulations

50. The college offered a variety of seminars to upperclassmen. 50.____
    The word *seminars,* as used in this sentence, means MOST NEARLY

    A. reading courses with no formal supervision
    B. study courses for small groups of students engaged in research under a teacher
    C. guidance conferences with grade advisors
    D. work experiences in different occupational fields

KEY (CORRECT ANSWERS)

1. C	11. D	21. C	31. A	41. C
2. C	12. A	22. C	32. B	42. C
3. A	13. B	23. B	33. D	43. B
4. D	14. C	24. B	34. C	44. A
5. B	15. C	25. A	35. B	45. D
6. C	16. C	26. C	36. A	46. C
7. D	17. B	27. C	37. B	47. B
8. A	18. D	28. D	38. A	48. B
9. C	19. C	29. C	39. D	49. C
10. A	20. D	30. A	40. A	50. B

WORD MEANING
EXAMINATION SECTION
TEST 1

DIRECTIONS: Each question or incomplete statement is followed by several suggested answers or completions. Select the one that BEST answers the question or completes the statement. *PRINT THE LETTER OF THE CORRECT ANSWER IN THE SPACE AT THE RIGHT.*

1. In the sentence, *Malice was immanent in all his remarks,* the word *immanent* means MOST NEARLY 1.____

   A. elevated
   B. inherent
   C. threatening
   D. foreign

2. In the sentence, *The extant copies of the document were found in the safe,* the word *extant* means MOST NEARLY 2.____

   A. existing
   B. original
   C. forged
   D. duplicate

3. In the sentence, *The recruit was more complaisant after the captain spoke to him,* the word *complaisant* means MOST NEARLY 3.____

   A. calm
   B. affable
   C. irritable
   D. confident

4. In the sentence, *The man was captured under highly creditable circumstances,* the word *creditable* means MOST NEARLY 4.____

   A. doubtful
   B. believable
   C. praiseworthy
   D. unexpected

5. In the sentence, *His superior officers were more sagacious than he,* the word *sagacious* means MOST NEARLY 5.____

   A. shrewd   B. obtuse   C. absurd   D. verbose

6. In the sentence, *He spoke with impunity,* the word *impunity* means MOST NEARLY 6.____

   A. rashness
   B. caution
   C. without fear
   D. immunity

7. In the sentence, *The new patrolman displayed unusual temerity during the emergency,* the word *temerity* means MOST NEARLY 7.____

   A. fear   B. rashness   C. calmness   D. anxiety

8. In the sentence, *The portions of food were parsimoniously served,* the word *parsimoniously* means MOST NEARLY 8.____

   A. stingily
   B. piously
   C. elaborately
   D. generously

103

9. In the sentence, *Generally the speaker's remarks were sententious,* the word *sententious* means MOST NEARLY

   A. verbose
   B. witty
   C. argumentative
   D. pithy

10. In the sentence, *The prisoner was fractious when brought to the station house,* the word *fractious* means MOST NEARLY

    A. penitent
    B. talkative
    C. irascible
    D. broken-hearted

11. In the sentence, *The judge was implacable when the attorney pleaded for leniency,* the word *implacable* means MOST NEARLY

    A. inexorable
    B. disinterested
    C. inattentive
    D. indifferent

12. In the sentence, *The court ordered the mendacious statements stricken from the record,* the word *mendacious* means MOST NEARLY

    A. begging
    B. lying
    C. threatening
    D. lengthy

13. In the sentence, *The district attorney spoke in a strident voice,* the word *strident* means MOST NEARLY

    A. loud
    B. harsh-sounding
    C. sing-song
    D. low

14. In the sentence, *The speaker had a predilection for long sentences,* the word *predilection* means MOST NEARLY

    A. aversion
    B. talent
    C. propensity
    D. diffidence

15. A section of the Penal Law states that *a morbid propensity to commit prohibited acts.... forms no defense to a prosecution therefor.*
    The word *propensity* as used in this statute means MOST NEARLY

    A. capacity   B. ability   C. tendency   D. aptitude

16. A police department rule provides that a *Chaplain shall have the assimilated rank of Inspector.*
    The word *assimilated* as used in this rule means MOST NEARLY

    A. false
    B. superior
    C. comparable
    D. presumed

17. A police department rule provides that *Pushcarts and derelict automobiles shall be delivered to the Bureau of Incumbrances.*
    The word *derelict* as used in this rule means MOST NEARLY

    A. dilapidated
    B. abandoned
    C. delinquent
    D. contraband

18. A police department rule provides that *when the exigencies of the service shall so require, a captain may assign a patrolman from the outgoing platoon to house duty.* The word *exigencies* as used in this rule means MOST NEARLY

    A. needs
    B. conveniences
    C. changes
    D. increases

19. A police department rule provides for the award of a Medal for Merit *for an act of outstanding bravery, performed in the line of duty, at imminent personal hazard of life.* The word *imminent* as used in this rule means MOST NEARLY

    A. impending
    B. inherent
    C. certain
    D. great

20. A police department rule provides that *the Police Commissioner shall have cognizance and control of the government, administration, disposition and discipline of the Police Department.*
    The word *cognizance* as used in this rule means MOST NEARLY

    A. responsibility for
    B. jurisdiction over
    C. knowledge of
    D. ability for

21. A police department rule provides that a member of the department shall not communicate with a railroad company *for the purpose of expediting the issue of a transportation pass.*
    The word *expediting* as used in this rule means MOST NEARLY

    A. extorting
    B. procuring
    C. demanding
    D. hastening

22. A section of the Penal Law provides, in part, that *whenever the punishment or penalty for an offense is mitigated by any provision of this chapter, such provision may be applied to any sentence or judgment imposed for the offense.*
    The word *mitigated* as used in this statute means MOST NEARLY

    A. removed
    B. augmented
    C. changed
    D. decreased

23. A Police Department Manual of Procedure provides that a member of the force who comes into possession of a document containing scurrilous matter will take precautions to safeguard fingerprints thereon.
    The word *scurrilous* as used in this regulation means MOST NEARLY

    A. irrelevant
    B. offensive
    C. defamatory
    D. evidentiary

24. Under cases of *Mendicancy* should be listed cases of

    A. loitering
    B. begging
    C. carrying of weapons
    D. injury to property

25. A police department rule states that *the Department Medal of Honor may be awarded to a member of the Force who distinguishes himself by an act of gallantry and intrepidity.*
    The word *intrepidity* as used in this rule means MOST NEARLY

    A. chivalry
    B. virility
    C. fear
    D. courage

KEY (CORRECT ANSWERS)

1. B
2. A
3. B
4. C
5. A

6. D
7. B
8. A
9. D
10. C

11. A
12. B
13. B
14. C
15. C

16. C
17. B
18. A
19. A
20. C

21. D
22. D
23. B
24. B
25. D

TEST 2

DIRECTIONS: Each question or incomplete statement is followed by several suggested answers or completions. Select the one that BEST answers the question or completes the statement. *PRINT THE LETTER OF THE CORRECT ANSWER IN THE SPACE AT THE RIGHT.*

1. A foreman who <u>expedites</u> a job   1.____
   - A. abolishes it
   - B. makes it bigger
   - C. slows it down
   - D. speeds it up

2. If a man is working at a <u>uniform</u> speed, it means he is working at a speed which is   2.____
   - A. changing
   - B. fast
   - C. slow
   - D. steady

3. To say that a caretaker is <u>obstinate</u> means that he is   3.____
   - A. cooperative
   - B. patient
   - C. stubborn
   - D. willing

4. To say that a caretaker is <u>negligent</u> means that he is   4.____
   - A. careless
   - B. neat
   - C. nervous
   - D. late

5. To say that something is <u>absurd</u> means that it is   5.____
   - A. definite
   - B. not clear
   - C. ridiculous
   - D. unfair

6. To say that a foreman is <u>impartial</u> means that he is   6.____
   - A. fair
   - B. improving
   - C. in a hurry
   - D. watchful

7. A foreman who is <u>lenient</u> is one who is   7.____
   - A. careless
   - B. harsh
   - C. inexperienced
   - D. mild

8. A foreman who is <u>punctual</u> is one who is   8.____
   - A. able
   - B. polite
   - C. prompt
   - D. sincere

9. If you think one of your men is too <u>awkward</u> to do a job, it means you think he is too   9.____
   - A. clumsy
   - B. lazy
   - C. old
   - D. weak

10. A man who is <u>seldom</u> late is late   10.____
    - A. always
    - B. never
    - C. often
    - D. rarely

Questions 11-18.

DIRECTIONS: In Questions 11 through 18, select the choice that is CLOSEST in meaning to the underlined word.

11. A central file eliminates the need to retain duplicate material.

    A. keep B. change C. locate D. process

12. Filing is a routine office task.

    A. proper B. regular C. simple D. difficult

13. Sometimes a word, phrase, or sentence must be deleted to correct an error.

    A. removed B. added C. expanded D. improved

14. Your supervisor will evaluate your work.

    A. judge B. list C. assign D. explain

15. Railroad Clerks must ascertain the identification of all individuals claiming to be Transit Authority employees.

    A. observe B. record C. challenge D. verify

16. A Railroad Clerk must not permit anyone to loiter near his booth.

    A. throw refuse
    B. smoke
    C. stand idly
    D. make noise

17. The Transit Authority has a program for eliminating graffiti in subway cars.

    A. noise
    B. markings
    C. vandalism
    D. debris

18. The Railroad Clerk will deduct the number of tokens she sold from the number of tokens she had in reserve when she started her tour of duty.

    A. add B. subtract C. multiply D. divide

Questions 19-30.

DIRECTIONS: Questions 19 through 30 contain incorrectly used words which change the meaning of the statement. Identify the word in the statement that is incorrect and select the choice that would make the sentence correct.

19. Lack of employee input in the case of training often exists, but is frequently dealt with in evaluation of the training effort. Failure to deal with as important a factor as this can be ruinous to the training effort.

    A. Seldom
    B. Margin
    C. Ancillary
    D. Contributory

20. It is a fallacy that policies generated at the top of the hierarchy are often not acceptable to those on the lower levels, particularly in the case of blue-collar workers among whom the rewards and sanctions of the union or members of the immediate social group are more impelling than the rewards or sanctions available to management.   20._____

    A. Parologism
    B. Truism
    C. Commands
    D. Undetermined

21. Basically, an organization develops when employees in it have rather free control over their behavior within the organization, when the philosophy of the organization is that maximum interpersonal interplay through a minimum number of hierarchical levels is desirable, and when a person traditionally called a *trainer* performs an integrating function.   21._____

    A. Instinctively
    B. Total
    C. Flat
    D. Strong

22. In gaining cooperation in human relations, the one who would influence must often foster his own ego and fertilize and feed that of the one who is to be influenced.   22._____

    A. Lassitude
    B. Emulate
    C. Suppress
    D. Implant

23. In the United States, in general, we have been criticized for our emphasis upon physical, materialistic, and economic goals. These are still important, but the trends point toward the more complex, or appreciation of the beautiful, as for example in the architecture of our new factories and colors in the workplaces.   23._____

    A. Ephemeral   B. Concrete   C. Prosaic   D. Aesthetic

24. Standards of production performance are necessary to reveal the quantities of material, the number of hours of labor, the machine hours, and quantities of service (as, for example, power, steam, etc.) necessary to perform the various production operations. The establishment of such standards is an engineering rather than an accounting task, but it should be emphasized that such standards are needless to the development of the budgetary procedure at least insofar as the budget is to serve as a tool of control. Such standards serve not only in the development of the budget and in measuring efficiency of production performance, but also in developing purchase requirements and in estimating costs.   24._____

    A. Manifest
    B. Evaluation
    C. Essential
    D. Function

25. Where standard costs are not available or their use is impracticable due to uncertainty of prices, estimates of the costs must be made on the basis of past experience and expected conditions. Ability to use standards largely eliminates the use of the budget for purposes of control of costs but its value remains for purposes of coordination of the program with purchases and finance.   25._____

    A. Failure
    B. Current
    C. Culmination
    D. Apparent

26. While one of the first objectives of the labor budget is to provide the highest practicable degree of regularity of employment, consideration must also be given to the estimating and perdurability of labor cost. Regularity of employment in itself effects some reduction in labor cost, but when carried beyond the point of practicability, it may increase other costs. For example, additional sales effort may be required to expand sales volume or to develop new products for slack periods; the cost of carrying inventories and the dangers of obsolescence and price declines must also be considered. A proper balance must be secured.

   A. Material   B. Control   C. Futures   D. To

27. The essentials of budgeting perhaps can be summarized in this manner:
   1. Develop a sound business program.
   2. Report on the progress in achieving that program.
   3. Take necessary action as to all variances which are inevitable.
   4. Revise the program to meet the changing conditions as required.

   A. Perfect   B. Plans
   C. Controllable   D. Secure

28. If a planning and control procedure is considered worthwhile, then it is a syllogism that preparation for the installation should be adequate. Time devoted to this educational aspect ordinarily will prove quite rewarding. The management to be involved with the budget, and particularly the middle management, must have a clear understanding of the budgetary procedure.

   A. Acquired   B. Remedial   C. Monetary   D. Truism

29. Among the Housing Manager's overall responsibilities in administering a project is the prevention of the development of conditions which might lead to termination of tenancy and eviction of a tenant. Where there appears to be doubt that a tenant is fully aware of his responsibilities and is thus jeopardizing his tenancy, the Housing Manager should acquaint him with these responsibilities. Where a situation involves behavior of a tenant or a member of his family, the Housing Manager should confirm, through discussions and referrals to social agencies, correction of the conditions before they reach a state where there is no alternative but termination proceedings.

   A. Coordinate   B. Identify
   C. Assert   D. Attempt

30. The one universal administrative complaint is that the budget is inadequate. Between adequacy and inadequacy lie all degrees of adequacy. Further, human wants are modest in relation to human resources. From these two facts we may conclude that the fundamental criterion of administrative decision must be a criterion of efficiency (the degree to which the goals have been reached relative to the available resources) rather than a criterion of adequacy (the degree to which its goals have been reached). The task of the manager is to maximize social values relative to limited resources.

   A. Improve   B. Simple
   C. Limitless   D. Optimize

KEY (CORRECT ANSWERS)

1.	D	16.	C
2.	D	17.	B
3.	C	18.	B
4.	A	19.	A
5.	C	20.	B
6.	A	21.	D
7.	D	22.	C
8.	C	23.	D
9.	A	24.	C
10.	D	25.	B
11.	A	26.	B
12.	B	27.	C
13.	A	28.	D
14.	A	29.	D
15.	D	30.	C

WORD MEANING

EXAMINATION SECTION
TEST 1

Questions 1-20.

DIRECTIONS: Each question consists of a statement. You are to indicate whether the statement is TRUE (T) or FALSE (F). *PRINT THE LETTER OF THE CORRECT ANSWER IN THE SPACE AT THE RIGHT.*

1. *To eliminate hand pumping* means NEARLY the same as *to do away with hand pumping.* 1._____

2. *Discarding a ladder with a cracked rung* means NEARLY the same as *repairing a ladder with a cracked rung.* 2._____

3. A *projecting* stub is USUALLY a stub which sticks out. 3._____

4. A *nitrogen deficiency* in the soil is an oversupply of nitrogen in the soil. 4._____

5. Saying that a soil has a heavy *texture* is NEARLY the same as saying that the soil has a deep color. 5._____

6. A *neutral* soil is one in which no useful plants will grow. 6._____

7. A plant which is *dormant* is USUALLY in an inactive period of growth. 7._____

8. Saying that sun is *detrimental* to ferns is NEARLY the same as saying that sun is harmful to ferns. 8._____

9. *Vendors are permitted only in certain park areas.* In this sentence, the word *vendors* means NEARLY the same as *sellers.* 9._____

10. *The Assistant Gardener was confident that he would be able to learn the new work quickly.* In this sentence, the word *confident* means NEARLY the same as *sure.* 10._____

11. *The employee's behavior on the job was improper.* In this sentence, the word *improper* means NEARLY the same as *good.* 11._____

12. *The foreman's oral instructions were always clear and to the point.* In this sentence, the word *oral* means NEARLY the same as *spoken.* 12._____

13. *A covering with paper will prevent excessive loss of moisture from the surface soil.* In this sentence, the word *excessive* means NEARLY the same as *unnecessary.* 13._____

14. *In making a permanent hotbed, the ground should be excavated to a depth of fifteen inches.* In this sentence, the word *excavated* means NEARLY the same as *dug out.* 14._____

15. *After the seed has been sown, an application of water will help it to germinate.* In this sentence, the word *germinate* means NEARLY the same as *start growing.* 15._____

16. *A sandy soil may be greatly improved through the incorporation of organic materials.* In this sentence, the word *incorporation* means NEARLY the same as *removal.* 16._____

17. *Manures are considered a concentrated form of fertilizer.* 17.____
In this sentence, the word *concentrated* means NEARLY the same as *natural*.

18. *Ventilation of some kind must be given the plants.* In this sentence, the word *ventilation* 18.____
means NEARLY the same as *heat*.

19. *When rain water enters soil, it penetrates air spaces.* In this sentence, the word *penetrates* means NEARLY the same as *fills*. 19.____

20. *The metal was corroded.* In this sentence, the word *corroded* means NEARLY the same as *polished*. 20.____

Questions 21-40.

DIRECTIONS: In answering Questions 21 through 40, select the lettered word which means MOST NEARLY the same as the capitalized word. *PRINT THE LETTER OF THE CORRECT ANSWER IN THE SPACE AT THE RIGHT.*

21. ACCURATE 21.____
 A. correct B. useful C. afraid D. careless

22. ALTER 22.____
 A. copy B. change C. repeat D. agree

23. DOCUMENT 23.____
 A. outline B. agreement C. blueprint D. record

24. INDICATE 24.____
 A. listen B. show C. guess D. try

25. INVENTORY 25.____
 A. custom B. discovery C. warning D. list

26. ISSUE 26.____
 A. annoy B. use up C. give out D. gain

27. NOTIFY 27.____
 A. inform B. promise C. approve D. strengthen

28. ROUTINE 28.____
 A. path B. mistake C. habit D. journey

29. TERMINATE 29.____
 A. rest B. start C. deny D. end

30. TRANSMIT 30.____
 A. put in B. send C. stop D. go across

3 (#1)

31. QUARANTINE
    - A. feed
    - B. keep separate
    - C. clean
    - D. give an injection to

    31.____

32. HERD
    - A. group
    - B. pair
    - C. person
    - D. ear

    32.____

33. SPECIES
    - A. few
    - B. favorite
    - C. kind
    - D. small

    33.____

34. INJURE
    - A. hurt
    - B. need
    - C. protect
    - D. help

    34.____

35. ANNOY
    - A. like
    - B. answer
    - C. rest
    - D. bother

    35.____

36. EXTINCT
    - A. likely
    - B. no longer exists
    - C. tired
    - D. gradually dying out

    36.____

37. CONFINE
    - A. fly about freely
    - B. free
    - C. keep within limits
    - D. care

    37.____

38. ENVIRONMENT
    - A. distant
    - B. surroundings
    - C. disease
    - D. lake

    38.____

39. AVIARY
    - A. pig pen
    - B. large bird cage
    - C. elephant cage
    - D. snake pit

    39.____

40. CRATE
    - A. make
    - B. report
    - C. box
    - D. truck

    40.____

KEY (CORRECT ANSWERS)

1.	T	11.	F	21.	A	31.	B
2.	F	12.	T	22.	B	32.	A
3.	T	13.	F	23.	D	33.	C
4.	F	14.	T	24.	B	34.	A
5.	F	15.	T	25.	D	35.	D
6.	F	16.	F	26.	C	36.	B
7.	T	17.	F	27.	A	37.	C
8.	T	18.	F	28.	C	38.	B
9.	T	19.	F	29.	D	39.	B
10.	T	20.	F	30.	B	40.	C

TEST 2

Questions 1-6.

DIRECTIONS: Questions 1 through 6 are to be answered on the basis of the following paragraph.

It is important that traffic signals be regularly and effectively maintained. Signals with impaired efficiency cannot be expected to command desired respect. Poorly maintained traffic signs create disrespect in the minds of those who are to obey them and thereby reduce the effectiveness and authority of the signs. Maintenance should receive paramount consideration in the design and purchase of traffic signal equipment. The initial step in a good maintenance program for traffic signals is the establishment of a maintenance record. This record should show the cost of operation and maintenance of different types of equipment. It should give complete information regarding signal operations and indicate where defective planning exists in maintenance programs.

1. The word *effectively*, as used in the above paragraph, means MOST NEARLY

   A. occasionally
   B. properly
   C. expensively
   D. cheaply

2. The word *impaired*, as used in the above paragraph, means MOST NEARLY

   A. reduced
   B. increased
   C. constant
   D. high

3. The word *desired*, as used in the above paragraph, means MOST NEARLY

   A. public
   B. complete
   C. wanted
   D. enough

4. The word *paramount*, as used in the above paragraph, means MOST NEARLY

   A. little
   B. chief
   C. excessive
   D. some

5. The word *initial*, as used in the above paragraph, means MOST NEARLY

   A. first
   B. final
   C. determining
   D. most important

6. The word *defective*, as used in the above paragraph, means MOST NEARLY

   A. suitable
   B. real
   C. good
   D. faulty

Questions 7-31.

DIRECTIONS: Each of Questions 7 through 31 consists of a capitalized word followed by four suggested meanings of the word. For each question, choose the word or phrase which means MOST NEARLY the same as the capitalized word.

7. ABOLISH

   A. count up
   B. do away with
   C. give more
   D. pay double for

8. ABUSE

   A. accept
   B. mistreat
   C. respect
   D. touch

9. ACCURATE
   A. correct   B. lost   C. neat   D. secret

10. ASSISTANCE
    A. attendance   B. belief
    C. help   D. reward

11. CAUTIOUS
    A. brave   B. careful   C. greedy   D. hopeful

12. COURTEOUS
    A. better   B. easy   C. polite   D. religious

13. CRITICIZE
    A. admit   B. blame   C. check on   D. make dirty

14. DIFFICULT
    A. capable   B. dangerous   C. dull   D. hard

15. ENCOURAGE
    A. aim at   B. beg for   C. cheer on   D. free from

16. EXTENT
    A. age   B. size   C. truth   D. wildness

17. EXTRAVAGANT
    A. empty   B. helpful   C. over   D. wasteful

18. FALSE
    A. absent   B. colored
    C. not enough   D. wrong

19. INDICATE
    A. point out   B. show up
    C. shrink from   D. take to

20. NEGLECT
    A. disregard   B. flatten
    C. likeness   D. thoughtfulness

21. PENALIZE
    A. make   B. notice   C. pay   D. punish

22. POSTPONED
    A. put off   B. repeated   C. taught   D. went to

23. PUNCTUAL

    A. bursting   B. catching
    C. make a hole in   D. on time

23.____

24. RARE

    A. large   B. ride up   C. unusual   D. young

24.____

25. REVEAL

    A. leave   B. renew   C. soften   D. tell

25.____

26. EXCESSIVE

    A. excusable   B. immoderate
    C. ethereal   D. intentional

26.____

27. VOLUNTARY

    A. common   B. paid   C. sharing   D. willing

27.____

28. WHOLESOME

    A. cheap   B. healthful   C. hot   D. together

28.____

29. SERIOUS

    A. important   B. order   C. sharp   D. tight

29.____

30. TRIVIAL

    A. alive   B. empty   C. petty   D. troublesome

30.____

31. VENTILATE

    A. air out   B. darken
    C. last   D. take a chance

31.____

Questions 32-40.

DIRECTIONS: Each question consists of a statement. You are to indicate whether the statement is TRUE (T) or FALSE (F).

32. *The price of this merchandise fluctuates from day to day.* In this sentence, the word *fluctuates* means the OPPOSITE of *remains steady*.

32.____

33. *The patient was in acute pain.* In this sentence, the word *acute* means the OPPOSITE of *slight*.

33.____

34. *The essential data appear in the report.* In this sentence, the word *data* means the OPPOSITE of *facts*.

34.____

35. *The open lounge is spacious.* In this sentence, the word *spacious* means the OPPOSITE of *well-lighted*.

35.____

36. *The landscaping work was a prolonged task.* In this sentence, the word *prolonged* means NEARLY the same as *difficult*.

36.____

37. *A transparent removable cover was placed over the flower bed.* In this sentence, the word *transparent* means NEARLY the same as *wooden*.

37.____

38. *The prompt action of the employee saved many lives.* In this sentence, the word *prompt* means NEARLY the same as *quick*.

38.____

39. *The attendant's request for a vacation was approved.* In this sentence, the word *approved* means NEARLY the same as *refused*.

39.____

40. *The paycheck was received in the mail.* In this sentence, the *word received* means NEARLY the same as *lost*.

40.____

KEY (CORRECT ANSWERS)

1.	B	11.	B	21.	D	31.	A
2.	A	12.	C	22.	A	32.	T
3.	C	13.	B	23.	D	33.	T
4.	B	14.	D	24.	C	34.	F
5.	A	15.	C	25.	D	35.	F
6.	D	16.	B	26.	B	36.	F
7.	B	17.	D	27.	D	37.	F
8.	B	18.	D	28.	B	38.	T
9.	A	19.	A	29.	A	39.	F
10.	C	20.	A	30.	C	40.	F

TEST 3

Questions 1-50.

DIRECTIONS: Each question consists of a statement. You are to indicate whether the statement is TRUE (T) or FALSE (F). *PRINT THE LETTER OF THE CORRECT ANSWER IN THE SPACE AT THE RIGHT.*

1. *A few men were assisting the attendant.* In this sentence, the word *assisting* means NEARLY the same as *helping*.   1.____

2. *He opposed the idea of using a vacuum cleaner for this job.* In this sentence, the word *opposed* means NEARLY the same as *suggested*.   2.____

3. *Four employees were selected.* In this sentence, the word *selected* means NEARLY the same as *chosen*.   3.____

4. *This man is constantly supervised.* In this sentence, the word *constantly* means NEARLY the same as *rarely*.   4.____

5. *One part of soap to two parts of water is sufficient.* In this sentence, the word *sufficient* means NEARLY the same as *enough*.   5.____

6. *The fire protection system was inadequate.* In this sentence, the word *inadequate* means NEARLY the same as *very good*.   6.____

7. *The nozzle of the hose was clogged.* In this sentence, the word *clogged* means NEARLY the same as *brass*.   7.____

8. *He resembles the man who worked here before.* In this sentence, the word *resembles* means NEARLY the same as *replaces*.   8.____

9. *They eliminated a number of items.* In this sentence, the word *eliminated* means NEARLY the same as *bought*.   9.____

10. *He is a dependable worker.* In this sentence, the word *dependable* means NEARLY the same as *poor*.   10.____

11. *Some wood finishes color the wood and conceal the natural grain.* In this sentence, the word *conceal* means NEARLY the same as *hide*.   11.____

12. *Paint that is chalking sometimes retains its protective value.* In this sentence, the word *retains* means NEARLY the same as *keeps*.   12.____

13. *Wood and trash had accumulated.* In this sentence, the word *accumulated* means NEARLY the same as *piled up*.   13.____

14. *An inflammable liquid is one that is easily set on fire.*   14.____

15. *The amounts were then compared.* In this sentence, the word *compared* means NEARLY the same as *added*.   15.____

2 (#3)

16. *The boy had fallen into a shallow pool.* In this sentence, the word *shallow* means NEARLY the same as *deep.* 16._____

17. *He acquired a new instrument.* In this sentence, the word *acquired* means NEARLY the same as *got.* 17._____

18. *Several men were designated for this activity.* In this sentence, the word *designated* means NEARLY the same as *laid off.* 18._____

19. *The drawer had been converted into a file.* In this sentence, the word *converted* means NEARLY the same as *changed.* 19._____

20. *The patient has recuperated.* In this sentence, the word *recuperated* means NEARLY the same as *died.* 20._____

21. *A rigid material should be used.* In this sentence, the word *rigid* means NEARLY the same as *stiff.* 21._____

22. *Only half the supplies were utilized.* In this sentence, the word *utilized* means NEARLY the same as *used.* 22._____

23. *In all these years, he had never obstructed any change.* In this sentence, the word *obstructed* means NEARLY the same as *suggested.* 23._____

24. *Conditions were aggravated when he left.* In this sentence, the word *aggravated* means NEARLY the same as *improved.* 24._____

25. *The autopsy room is now available.* In this sentence, the word *available* means NEARLY the same as *clean.* 25._____

26. *An investigation which precedes a report is one which comes before the report.* 26._____

27. *Another word was inserted.* In this sentence, the word *inserted* means NEARLY the same as *put in.* 27._____

28. *He reversed the recommended steps in the procedure.* In this sentence, the word *reversed* means NEARLY the same as *explained.* 28._____

29. *His complaint was about a trivial matter.* In this sentence, the word *trivial* means NEARLY the same as *petty.* 29._____

30. *Using the proper tool will aid a worker in doing a better job.* In this sentence, the word *aid* means NEARLY the same as *help.* 30._____

31. *The application form has a space for the name of the former employer.* In this sentence, the word *former* means NEARLY the same as *new.* 31._____

32. *The exterior of the building needed to be painted.* In this sentence, the word *exterior* means NEARLY the same as *inside.* 32._____

33. *The smoke from the fire was dense.* In this sentence, the word *dense* means NEARLY the same as *thick.* 33._____

34. *Vacations should be planned in advance.* In this sentence, vacations should be planned ahead of time.   34.____

35. *The employee denied that he would accept another job.*   35.____
    In this sentence, the word *denied* means NEARLY the same as *admitted*.

36. *An annual report is made by the central stockroom.* In this sentence, the word annual means NEARLY the same as *monthly*.   36.____

37. *Salaries were increased in the new budget.* In this sentence, the word *increased* means NEARLY the same as *cut*.   37.____

38. *All excess oil is to be removed from tools.* In this sentence, the word *excess* means NEARLY the same as *extra*.   38.____

39. *The new employee did similar work on his last job.* In this sentence, the word *similar* means NEARLY the same as *interesting*.   39.____

40. *Helpful employees make favorable impressions on the public.* In this sentence, the word *favorable* means NEARLY the same as *poor*.   40.____

41. *Some plants are grown for the decorative value of their leaves.* In this sentence, the word *decorative* means NEARLY the same as *ornamental*.   41.____

42. *They made a circular flower garden.* In this sentence, the word *circular* means NEARLY the same as *square*.   42.____

43. *The gardener was a conscientious worker.* In this sentence, the word *conscientious* means NEARLY the same as *lazy*.   43.____

44. *The instructions received were contradictory.* In this sentence, the word *contradictory* means NEARLY the same as *alike*.   44.____

45. *His application for the job was rejected.* In this sentence, the word *rejected* means NEARLY the same as *accepted*.   45.____

46. *This plant reaches maturity quickly.* In this sentence, the word *maturity* means NEARLY the same as *full development*.   46.____

47. *The garden was provided with a system of underground irrigation.* In this sentence, the word *irrigation* means NEARLY the same as *watering*.   47.____

48. *In some plants, the flowers often appear before the foliage.* In this sentence, the word *foliage* refers to the leaves of the plant.   48.____

49. *The new horticultural society was organized through the merger of two previous groups.*   49.____
    In this sentence, the word *merger* means NEARLY the same as *breakup*.

50. *The stem of the plant measured three inches in diameter.* In this sentence, the word *diameter* means NEARLY the same as *height*.   50.____

KEY (CORRECT ANSWERS)

1. T	11. T	21. T	31. F	41. T
2. F	12. T	22. T	32. F	42. F
3. T	13. T	23. F	33. T	43. F
4. F	14. T	24. F	34. T	44. F
5. T	15. F	25. F	35. F	45. F
6. F	16. F	26. T	36. F	46. T
7. F	17. T	27. T	37. F	47. T
8. F	18. F	28. F	38. T	48. T
9. F	19. T	29. T	39. F	49. F
10. F	20. F	30. T	40. F	50. F

ARITHMETIC

EXAMINATION SECTION
TEST 1

DIRECTIONS: Each question or incomplete statement is followed by several suggested answers or completions. Select the one that BEST answers the question or completes the statement. *PRINT THE LETTER OF THE CORRECT ANSWER IN THE SPACE AT THE RIGHT.*

1. From 30983 subtract 29998. The answer should be 1.____
   A. 985 B. 995 C. 1005 D. 1015

2. From $2537.75 subtract $1764.28. The answer should be 2.____
   A. $763.58 B. $773.47 C. $774.48 D. $873.58

3. From 254211 subtract 76348. The answer should be 3.____
   A. 177863 B. 177963 C. 187963 D. 188973

4. Divide 4025 by 35. The answer should be 4.____
   A. 105 B. 109 C. 115 D. 125

5. Multiply 0.35 by 2764. The answer should be 5.____
   A. 997.50 B. 967.40 C. 957.40 D. 834.40

6. Multiply 1367 by 0.50. The answer should be 6.____
   A. 6.8350 B. 68.350 C. 683.50 D. 6835.0

7. Multiply 841 by 0.01. The answer should be 7.____
   A. 0.841 B. 8.41 C. 84.1 D. 841

8. Multiply 1962 by 25. The answer should be 8.____
   A. 47740 B. 48460 C. 48950 D. 49050

9. Multiply 905 by 0.05. The answer should be 9.____
   A. 452.5 B. 45.25 C. 4.525 D. 0.4525

10. Multiply 8.93 by 4.7. The answer should be 10.____
    A. 41.971 B. 40.871 C. 4.1971 D. 4.0871

11. Multiply 25 by 763. The answer should be 11.____
    A. 18075 B. 18875 C. 19075 D. 20965

12. Multiply 2530 by 0.10. The answer should be 12.____
    A. 2.5300 B. 25.300 C. 253.00 D. 2530.0

13. Multiply 3053 by 0.25. The answer should be   13.____
    A. 76.325   B. 86.315   C. 763.25   D. 863.15

14. Multiply 6204 by 0.35. The answer should be   14.____
    A. 2282.40   B. 2171.40   C. 228.24   D. 217.14

15. Multiply $.35 by 7619. The answer should be   15.____
    A. $2324.75   B. $2565.65   C. $2666.65   D. $2756.75

16. Multiply 6513 by 45. The answer should be   16.____
    A. 293185   B. 293085   C. 292185   D. 270975

17. Multiply 3579 by 70. The answer should be   17.____
    A. 25053.0   B. 240530   C. 250530   D. 259530

18. A class had an average of 24 words correct on a spelling test. The class average on this   18.____
    spelling test was 80%.
    The AVERAGE number of words missed on this test was
    A. 2   B. 4   C. 6   D. 8

19. In which one of the following is 24 renamed as a product of primes?   19.____
    A. 2 x 6 x 2   B. 8 x 3 x 1
    C. 2 x 2 x 3 x 2   D. 3 x 4 x 2

Questions 20-23.

DIRECTIONS: In answering Questions 20 through 23, perform the indicated operation. Select the BEST answer from the choices below.

20. Add: 7068   20.____
          2807
          9434
          6179
    A. 26,488   B. 24,588   C. 25,488   D. 25,478

21. Divide: 75√45555   21.____
    A. 674   B. 607.4   C. 6074   D. 60.74

22. Multiply: 907   22.____
              x806
    A. 73,142   B. 13,202   C. 721,042   D. 731,042

23. Subtract: 60085   23.____
              -47194
    A. 12,891   B. 13,891   C. 12,991   D. 12,871

24. A librarian reported that 1/5% of all books taken out last school year had not been returned.
    If 85,000 books were borrowed from the library, how many were not returned?   24._____

    A. 170   B. 425   C. 1,700   D. 4,250

25. At 40 miles per hour, how many minutes would it take to travel 12 miles?   25._____

    A. 30   B. 18   C. 15   D. 20

KEY (CORRECT ANSWERS)

1. A
2. B
3. A
4. C
5. B

6. C
7. B
8. D
9. B
10. A

11. C
12. C
13. C
14. B
15. C

16. B
17. C
18. C
19. C
20. C

21. B
22. D
23. A
24. A
25. B

SOLUTIONS TO PROBLEMS

1. 30,983 - 29,998 = 985

2. $2537.75 - $1764.28 = $773.47

3. 254,211 - 76,348 = 177,863

4. 4025 ÷ 35 = 115

5. (.35)(2764) = 967.4

6. (1367)(.50) = 683.5

7. (841)(.01) = 8.41

8. (1962)(25) = 49,050

9. (905)(.05) = 45.25

10. (8.93)(4.7) = 41.971

11. (25)(763) = 19,075

12. (2530)(.10) = 253

13. (3053)(.25) = 763.25

14. (6204)(.35) = 2171.4

15. ($.35)(7619) = $2666.65

16. (6513)(45) = 293,085

17. (3579)(70) = 250,530

18. 24 ÷ .80 = 30. Then, 30 - 24 = 6 words

19. 24 = 2 x 2 x 3 x 2, where each number is a prime.

20. 7068 ÷ 2807 + 9434 + 6179 = 25,488

21. 45,555 ÷ 75 = 607.4

22. (907)(806) = 731,042

23. 60,085 - 47,194 = 12,891

24. (1/5%)(85,000) = (.002)(85,000) = 170 books

25. Let x = number of minutes. Then, $\frac{40}{60} = \frac{12}{x}$. Solving, x = 18

TEST 2

DIRECTIONS: Each question or incomplete statement is followed by several suggested answers or completions. Select the one that BEST answers the question or completes the statement. *PRINT THE LETTER OF THE CORRECT ANSWER IN THE SPACE AT THE RIGHT.*

1. The sum of 57901 + 34762 is   1._____
   A.   81663   B.   82663   C.   91663   D.   92663

2. The sum of 559 + 448 + 362 + 662 is   2._____
   A.   2121   B.   2031   C.   2021   D.   1931

3. The sum of 36153 + 28624 + 81379 is   3._____
   A.   136156   B.   146046   C.   146146   D.   146156

4. The sum of 742 + 9197 + 8972 is   4._____
   A.   19901   B.   18911   C.   18801   D.   17921

5. The sum of 7989 + 8759 + 2726 is   5._____
   A.   18455   B.   18475   C.   19464   D.   19474

6. The sum of $111.55 + $95.05 + $38.80 is   6._____
   A. $234.40   B. $235.30   C. $245.40   D. $254.50

7. The sum of 1302 + 46187 + 92610 + 4522 is   7._____
   A.   144621   B.   143511   C.   134621   D.   134521

8. The sum of 47953 + 58041 + 63022 + 22333 is   8._____
   A.   170248   B.   181349   C.   191349   D.   200359

9. The sum of 76563 + 43693 + 38521 + 50987 + 72723 is   9._____
   A.   271378   B.   282386   C.   282487   D.   292597

10. The sum of 85923 + 97211 + 11333 + 4412 + 22533 is   10._____
    A.   209302   B.   212422   C.   221412   D.   221533

11. The sum of 4299 + 54163 + 89765 + 1012 + 38962 is   11._____
    A.   188201   B.   188300   C.   188301   D.   189311

12. The sum of 48526 + 709 + 11534 + 80432 + 6096 is   12._____
    A.   135177   B.   139297   C.   147297   D.   149197

13. The sum of $407.62 + $109.01 + $68.44 + $378.68 is   13._____
    A. $963.75   B. $964.85   C. $973.65   D. $974.85

14. From 40614 subtract 4697. The answer should be   14.____
    A. 35917   B. 35927   C. 36023   D. 36027

15. From 81773 subtract 5717. The answer should be   15.____
    A. 75964   B. 76056   C. 76066   D. 76956

16. From $1755.35 subtract $1201.75. The answer should be   16.____
    A. $542.50   B. $544.50   C. $553.60   D. $554.60

17. From $2402.10 subtract $998.85. The answer should be   17.____
    A. $1514.35   B. $1504.25   C. $1413.25   D. $1403.25

18. Add: 12 1/2   18.____
           2 1/2
           3 1/2
    A. 17   B. 17 1/4   C. 17 3/4   D. 18

19. Subtract: 150   19.____
                -80
    A. 70   B. 80   C. 130   D. 150

20. After cleaning up some lots in the city dump, five cleanup crews loaded the following   20.____
    amounts of garbage on trucks:
        Crew No. 1 loaded 2 1/4 tons
        Crew No. 2 loaded 3 tons
        Crew No. 3 loaded 1 1/4 tons
        Crew No. 4 loaded 2 1/4 tons
        Crew No. 5 loaded 1/2 ton.
    The TOTAL number of tons of garbage loaded was
    A. 8 1/4   B. 8 3/4   C. 9   D. 9 1/4

21. Subtract: 17 3/4   21.____
                -7 1/4
    A. 7 1/2   B. 10 1/2   C. 14 1/4   D. 17 3/4

22. Yesterday, Tom and Bill each received 10 leaflets about rat control. They were supposed   22.____
    to distribute one leaflet to each supermarket in the neighborhood. When the day was
    over, Tom had 8 leaflets left. Bill had no leaflets left.
    How many supermarkets got leaflets yesterday?
    A. 8   B. 10   C. 12   D. 18

23. What is 2/3 of 1 1/8?   23.____
    A. 1 11/16   B. 3/4   C. 3/8   D. 4 1/3

24. A farmer bought a load of 120 bushels of corn.   24.____
    After he fed 45 bushels to his hogs, what fraction of his supply remained?
    A. 5/8   B. 3/5   C. 3/8   D. 4/7

25. In the numeral 3,159,217, the 2 is in the _____ column.   25._____

    A. hundreds   B. units   C. thousands   D. tens

KEY (CORRECT ANSWERS)

1.	D	11.	A
2.	B	12.	C
3.	D	13.	A
4.	B	14.	A
5.	D	15.	B
6.	C	16.	C
7.	A	17.	D
8.	C	18.	D
9.	C	19.	A
10.	C	20.	D

21. B
22. C
23. B
24. A
25. A

SOLUTIONS TO PROBLEMS

1. 57,901 + 34,762 = 92,663

2. 559 + 448 + 362 + 662 = 2031

3. 36,153 + 28,624 + 81,379 = 146,156

4. 742 + 9197 + 8972 = 18,911

5. 7989 + 8759 + 2726 = 19,474

6. $111.55 + $95.05 + $38.80 = $245.40

7. 1302 + 46,187 + 92,610 + 4522 = 144,621

8. 47,953 + 58,041 + 63,022 + 22,333 = 191,349

9. 76,563 + 45,693 + 38,521 + 50,987 + 72,723 = 282,487

10. 85,923 + 97,211 + 11,333 + 4412 + 22,533 = 221,412

11. 4299 + 54,163 + 89,765 + 1012 + 38,962 = 188,201

12. 48,526 + 709 + 11,534 + 80,432 + 6096 = 147,297

13. $407.62 + $109.01 + $68.44 + $378.68 = $963.75

14. 40,614 - 4697 = 35,917

15. 81,773 - 5717 = 76,056

16. $1755.35 - $1201.75 = $553.60

17. $2402.10 - $998.85 = $1403.25

18. 12 1/2 + 2 1/4 + 3 1/4 = 17 4/4 = 18

19. 150 - 80 = 70

20. 2 1/4 + 3 + 1 1/4 + 2 1/4 + 1/2 = 8 5/4 = 9 1/4 tons

21. 17 3/4 - 7 1/4 = 10 2/4 = 10 1/2

22. 10 + 10 - 8 - 0 = 12 supermarkets

23. $(\frac{2}{3})(1\frac{1}{8}) = (\frac{2}{3})(\frac{9}{8}) = \frac{18}{24} = \frac{3}{4}$

24. 120 - 45 = 75. Then, $\frac{75}{120} = \frac{5}{8}$

25. The number 2 is in the hundreds column of 3,159,217

TEST 3

DIRECTIONS: Each question or incomplete statement is followed by several suggested answers or completions. Select the one that BEST answers the question or completes the statement. *PRINT THE LETTER OF THE CORRECT ANSWER IN THE SPACE AT THE RIGHT.*

1. The distance covered in three minutes by a subway train traveling at 30 mph is _____ mile(s).

    A. 3 B. 2 C. 1 1/2 D. 1

2. A crate contains 3 pieces of equipment weighing 73, 84, and 47 pounds, respectively. The empty crate weighs 16 pounds.
   If the crate is lifted by 4 trackmen, each trackman lifting one corner of the crate, the AVERAGE number of pounds lifted by each of the trackmen is

    A. 68 B. 61 C. 55 D. 51

3. The weight per foot of a length of square-bar 4" x 4" in cross-section, as compared with one 2" x 2" in cross-section, is _____ as much.

    A. twice B. 2 1/2 times
    C. 3 times D. 4 times

4. An order for 360 feet of 2" x 8" lumber is shipped in 20-foot lengths.
   The MAXIMUM number of 9-foot pieces that can be cut from this shipment is

    A. 54 B. 40 C. 36 D. 18

5. If a trackman gets $10.40 per hour and time and one-half for working over 40 hours, his gross salary for a week in which he worked 44 hours should be

    A. $457.60 B. $478.40 C. $499.20 D. $514.80

6. If a section of ballast 6'-0" wide, 8'-0" long, and 2'-6" deep is excavated, the amount of ballast removed is _____ cu. feet.

    A. 96 B. 104 C. 120 D. 144

7. The sum of 7'2 3/4", 0'-2 7/8", 3'-0", 4'-6 3/8", and 1'-9 1/4" is

    A. 16'-8 1/4" B. 16'-8 3/4" C. 16'-9 1/4" D. 16'-9 3/4"

8. The sum of 3 1/16", 4 1/4", 2 5/8", and 5 7/16" is

    A. 15 3/16" B. 15 1/4" C. 15 3/8" D. 15 1/2"

9. Add: $51.79, $29.39, and $8.98.
   The CORRECT answer is

    A. $78.97 B. $88.96 C. $89.06 D. $90.16

10. Add: $72.07 and $31.54. Then subtract $25.75.
    The CORRECT answer is

    A. $77.86 B. $82.14 C. $88.96 D. $129.36

11. Start with $82.47. Then subtract $25.50, $4.75, and 35¢. 11.____
    The CORRECT answer is

    A. $30.60   B. $51.87   C. $52.22   D. $65.25

12. Add: $19.35 and $37.75. Then subtract $9.90 and $19.80. 12.____
    The CORRECT answer is

    A. $27.40   B. $37.00   C. $37.30   D. $47.20

13. Add: $153 13.____
           114
           210
          +186

    A. $657   B. $663   C. $713   D. $757

14. Add: $64.91 14.____
           13.53
           19.27
           20.00
          +72.84

    A. $170.25   B. $178.35   C. $180.45   D. $190.55

15. Add: 1963 15.____
           1742
          +2497

    A. 6202   B. 6022   C. 5212   D. 5102

16. Add: 206 16.____
           709
           1342
          +2076

    A. 3432   B. 3443   C. 4312   D. 4333

17. Subtract: $190.76 17.____
              -   .99

    A. $189.97   B. $189.87   C. $189.77   D. $189.67

18. From 99876 subtract 85397. The answer should be 18.____

    A. 14589   B. 14521   C. 14479   D. 13589

19. From $876.51 subtract $92.89. The answer should be 19.____

    A. $773.52   B. $774.72   C. $783.62   D. $784.72

20. From 70935 subtract 49489. The answer should be 20.____

    A. 20436   B. 21446   C. 21536   D. 21546

21. From $391.55 subtract $273.45. The answer should be   21._____
    A. $118.10   B. $128.20   C. $178.10   D. $218.20

22. When 119 is subtracted from the sum of 2016 + 1634, the answer is   22._____
    A. 2460   B. 3531   C. 3650   D. 3769

23. Multiply 35 x 65 x 15. The answer should be   23._____
    A. 2275   B. 24265   C. 31145   D. 34125

24. Multiply: 4.06   24._____
               x.031
    A. 1.2586   B. .12586   C. .02586   D. .1786

25. When 65 is added to the result of 14 multiplied by 13, the answer is   25._____
    A. 92   B. 182   C. 247   D. 16055

KEY (CORRECT ANSWERS)

1. C   11. B
2. C   12. A
3. D   13. B
4. C   14. D
5. B   15. A

6. C   16. D
7. C   17. C
8. C   18. C
9. D   19. C
10. A   20. B

21. A
22. B
23. D
24. B
25. C

SOLUTIONS TO PROBLEMS

1. Let x = distance. Then, $\dfrac{30}{60} = \dfrac{x}{3}$ Solving, x = 1 1/2 miles

2. (73 + 84 + 47 + 16) ÷ 4 = 55 pounds

3. (4 x 4) ÷ (2 x 2) = a ratio of 4 to 1.

4. 20 ÷ 9 = 2 2/9, rounded down to 2 pieces. Then, (360 ÷ 20)(2) = 36

5. Salary = ($10.40)(40) + ($15.60)(4) = $478.40

6. (6)(8)(2 1/2) = 120 cu.ft.

7. $7'2\dfrac{3}{4}" + 0'2\dfrac{7}{8}" + 3'0" + 4'6\dfrac{3}{8}" + 1'9\dfrac{1}{4}" = 15'19\dfrac{18}{8}" = 15'21\dfrac{1}{4}" = 16'9\dfrac{1}{4}"$

8. $3\dfrac{1}{16}" + 4\dfrac{1}{4}" + 2\dfrac{5}{8}" + 5\dfrac{7}{16}" = 14\dfrac{22}{16}" = 15\dfrac{3}{8}"$

9. $51.79 + $29.39 + $8.98 = $90.16

10. $72.07 + $31.54 = $103.61. Then, $103.61 - $25.75 = $77.86

11. $82.47 - $25.50 - $4.75 - $0.35 = $51.87

12. $19.35 + $37.75 = $57.10. Then, $57.10 - $9.90 - $19.80 = $27.40

13. $153 + $114 + $210 + $186 = $663

14. $64.91 + $13.53 + $19.27 + $20.00 + $72.84 = $190.55

15. 1963 + 1742 + 2497 = 6202

16. 206 + 709 + 1342 + 2076 = 4333

17. $190.76 - .99 = $189.77

18. 99,876 - 85,397 = 14,479

19. $876.51 - $92.89 = $783.62

20. 70,935 - 49,489 = 21,446

21. $391.55 - $273.45 = $118.10

22. (2016 + 1634) - 119 = 3650 - 119 = 3531

23. (35)(65)(15) = 34,125

24. (4.06)(.031) = .12586

25. 65 + (14)(13) = 65 + 182 = 247

ARITHMETICAL REASONING
EXAMINATION SECTION
TEST 1

DIRECTIONS: Each question or incomplete statement is followed by several suggested answers or completions. Select the one that BEST answers the question or completes the Statement. *PRINT THE LETTER OF THE CORRECT ANSWER IN THE SPACE AT THE RIGHT.*

1. The weekly pay for 8 hours a day, 5 days a week, at $16.8750 an hour can be calculated as

    A. 5 x 8 x 16.8570
    B. 8 + 5 x 16.8750
    C. 8 x 5 x 16.8750
    D. 8 + 5 x 16.8570

2. A bus operator starts out with $10.00 in change, and his fare box indicates he collects $85.50 in passenger fares. On counting his money, he finds he has 75 one dollar bills, 10 fifty cent pieces, 22 quarters, and 70 dimes.
   To have the CORRECT amount, the number of nickels he should have is

    A. 45   B. 50   C. 55   D. 60

3. The register on the fare box of a certain bus has 5 dials and shows the total number of cents collected. When a particular bus operator starts his tour of duty, the register reading is 08980, and at the conclusion of his tour of duty the reading is 14540.
   The TOTAL number of 20-cent fares collected during this operator's tour was

    A. 278   B. 598   C. 783   D. 969

4. A particular bus has 12 cross seats holding two passengers each, plus rear and longitudinal seats holding a total of 14 additional passengers.
   If the number of standees permitted on a bus is one-half the number of seated passengers, the TOTAL passenger capacity of this bus is

    A. 26   B. 38   C. 39   D. 57

5. A crosstown bus operates between two terminals 22 blocks apart and makes 18 stops. It takes half a minute to travel each block and a quarter of a minute at each stop, and 5 minutes are lost at traffic lights.
   The TOTAL time required to go from one terminal to the other is _____ minutes.

    A. 15 1/2   B. 17 1/2   C. 20 1/2   D. 22 1/2

6. The TOTAL value of an operator's change fund consisting of 7 half-dollars, 19 quarters, 169 dimes, and 105 nickels is

    A. $28.40   B. $29.40   C. $30.40   D. $31.40

7. If it takes a bus 30 seconds to pass two checkpoints that are 500 feet apart, then the speed of the bus is APPROXIMATELY _____ m.p.h.

    A. 10.1   B. 11.4   C. 12.7   D. 14.2

8. If the length of a particular bus route is 8.6 miles and the average speed of a bus on this route is 7.5 miles per hour, then the ONE-WAY running time for a bus is _____ minutes.

   A. 52.3   B. 64.5   C. 68.8   D. 75.6

9. If your watch gains 20 minutes per day and you set it to the correct time at 7:00 A.M., the correct time, to the NEAREST minute, when the watch indicates 1:00 P.M. is

   A. 12:50   B. 12:56   C. 1:05   D. 1:10

10. A particular bus seats 34 passengers and stands half that number.
    The TOTAL passenger capacity of the bus is

    A. 41   B. 51   C. 61   D. 68

11. The fare register box on a bus shows the total number of cents collected. At the beginning of a run, the register reading of a certain box was 15750 and at the end of the run the reading was 17150.
    The TOTAL number of $1.00 fares collected during the run was

    A. 16   B. 17   C. 14   D. 19

12. Manuals on driving stress the importance of allowing ample braking distance to the car ahead, the most common rule of thumb being to allow a car length for each ten miles per hour of speed.
    If the overall length of a car is 210 inches, the proper braking distance to allow at a speed of 40 miles per hour is NEAREST to _____ feet.

    A. 700   B. 500   C. 70   D. 50

13. A bus requires 40 minutes to go from one terminal to another and stops for 10 minutes at each terminal. The MAXIMUM number of one-way trips that the bus can complete in 6 hours is

    A. 6   B. 7   C. 8   D. 9

Questions 14-21.

DIRECTIONS: Questions 14 through 21 in Column I are questions of simple arithmetic, each of which has one of the answers listed in Column II. For each item in Column I, select the CORRECT answer from Column II.

COLUMN I	COLUMN II
14. 229 times 9	A. 1,383
15. 11,064 divided by 8	B. 1,752
16. 1,384 plus 368	C. 2,061
17. 3,021 minus 447 minus 386	D. 2,682
18. 149 times 3 times 6	E. 2,188
19. 727 plus 17 plus 639	

20. 2,881 minus 693   20._____

21. 43,281 divided by 3 divided by 7   21._____

Questions 22-25.

DIRECTIONS: Questions 22 through 25 in Column I are questions of simple arithmetic, each of which has one of the answers listed in Column II. For each item in Column I, select the CORRECT answer from Column II.

COLUMN I	COLUMN II	
22. 198 times 3 times 4	A. 1,267	22._____
23. 837 plus 18 plus 412	B. 2,376	23._____
24. 8,869 divided by 7	C. 1,944	24._____
25. 2,693 minus 509	D. 1,867	25._____
	E. 2,184	
	F. 2,076	

KEY (CORRECT ANSWERS)

1. C   11. C
2. D   12. C
3. A   13. B
4. D   14. C
5. C   15. A

6. C   16. B
7. B   17. E
8. C   18. D
9. B   19. A
10. B 20. E

21. C
22. B
23. A
24. A
25. E

SOLUTIONS TO PROBLEMS

1. Weekly pay = 5 x 8 x 16.8750
2. $10.00 + $85.50 - ($75+$5+5.50+$7) = $3 = 60 nickels
3. 14,540 - 08980 = 05560, and 5560 ÷ 20 = 278
4. Number of people sitting = (12)(2) + 14 = 38. Number of people on bus = 38 + (1/2)(38) = 57
5. Total time = (22)(1/2) + (18)(1/4) + 5 = 20.5 minutes
6. (7)(.50) + (19)(.25) + (169)(.10) + (105)(.05) = $30.40
7. 500 ft in 30 sec = 16 2/3 ft per sec. Since 60 mph = 88 ft per sec, the bus' speed = (60)(16 2/3/88) 11.4 mph
8. Let x = number of minutes. Then, 7.5/60 = 8.6/x. Solving, x = 68.8
9. If the watch gains 20 mins. in 24 hrs., it gains 5/6 min. or 50 seconds in 1 hour. In 6 hours, from 7:00 AM to 1:00 PM, it gains 5 mins: (6 x 5/6). When the watch indicates 1:00 PM, the correct time is 12:55 PM.
10. Passenger capacity = 34 + (1/2)(34) = 51
11. 17150 - 15750 = 1400, so 1400 cents = 14 $1 fares
12. (210 in.)(40/10) = 840 in. = 70 ft.
13. 6 hrs. ÷ 5/6 hr. = 7.2, so 7 trips would be the maximum number.
14. (229)(9) = 2061
15. 11,064 ÷ 8 = 1383
16. 1384 + 368 = 1752
17. 3021 - 447 - 386 = 2188
18. (149)(3)(6) = 2682
19. 727 + 17 + 639 = 1383
20. 2881 - 693 = 2188
21. 43,281 ÷ 3 ÷ 7 = 2061
22. (198)(3)(4) = 2376
23. 837 + 18 + 412 = 1267
24. 8869 ÷ 7 = 1267
25. 2693 - 509 = 2184

TEST 2

DIRECTIONS: Each question or incomplete statement is followed by several suggested answers or completions. Select the one that BEST answers the question or completes the statement. *PRINT THE LETTER OF THE CORRECT ANSWER IN THE SPACE AT THE RIGHT.*

1. A bus depot took in $308,645.00 during a 3-month period. During the following 3-month period, the revenue decreased 17%.
   The revenue for the second 3-month period was MOST NEARLY

   A. $333,890.00 B. $283,400.00
   C. $256,175.00 D. $238,655.00

2. A surface line dispatcher desires to check the speed of a certain bus.
   If he times the bus as traveling 220 feet in 4.9 seconds, then the bus is traveling at APPROXIMATELY_____ m.p.h.

   A. 20   B. 30   C. 36   D. 44

3. If the thickness of material worn from a bus brake lining is approximately .20 inch for every 3,000 miles of wheel travel, then the number of miles the wheel will have traveled to reduce the thickness from .75 inch to .25 inch is

   A. 3,750   B. 6,000   C. 7,500   D. 11,250

4. A dispatcher desires to check the speed of a certain 40-foot bus.
   If he times the bus as passing him in 1.5 seconds, then the bus is traveling at APPROXIMATELY_____ m.p.h.

   A. 15   B. 18   C. 22   D. 27

5. The number of feet required to bring a bus traveling at 30 m.p.h. to a stop at a braking rate of 3 miles per hour per second is NEAREST to _____ feet.

   A. 180   B. 200   C. 220   D. 240

6. A bus leaves one time point at 10:35 and arrives at the next time point at 11:00.
   If the distance between the time points is 3 miles, the average speed of the bus, in m.p.h., was MOST NEARLY

   A. 6   B. 6 1/2   C. 7   D. 7 1/2

7. Eighty percent of the 300 operators in your depot are married, and 50% of all operators are under 35 years of age.
   The MINIMUM number of married operators in this lower age group is

   A. 60   B. 90   C. 150   D. 240

8. A bus maintained a speed of 5 m.p.h. for one-third of its route, 10 m.p.h. for the second third, and 15 m.p.h. for the final third.
   The AVERAGE speed for the entire route was CLOSEST to _____ m.p.h.

   A. 8   B. 9   C. 10   D. 11

9. During the month of August, approximately 900,000 more passengers used the surface lines than during the same month the year before. This was an increase of about 3%. The total number of passengers who used this surface transportation system during August was NEAREST to

   A. 3,000,000 B. 3,900,000
   C. 29,000,000 D. 31,000,000

10. Assume that there are 300 bus operators at terminal A. Terminal B has 85% as many bus operators as terminal A, and terminal C has 90% as many bus operators as terminal B. The number of operators assigned to terminal C is NEAREST to

    A. 230   B. 245   C. 255   D. 270

11. A bus leaves the terminal on time at 11:48 A.M. and after one roundtrip returns 11 minutes late at 1:06 P.M. It leaves again on time at 1:12 P.M.
    If the scheduled recovery time at both ends of the line is the same, the scheduled terminal-to-terminal running time, in minutes, is

    A. 25   B. 33   C. 42   D. 50

12. A bus line had a schedule headway of 6 minutes. Run #7 left the near terminal at 10:45 A.M. and shortly thereafter had to be taken out of service on account of engine trouble. Its passengers were picked up by its follower, run #8. The delay caused run #8 to arrive at the far terminal 6 minutes late.
    If the time of arrival of run #8 was 11:53 A.M., then the scheduled running time for the trip was _____ minutes.

    A. 44   B. 56   C. 68   D. 96

13. If a fuel storage tank contains 11,200 gallons of fuel when it is 85% full, its MAXIMUM capacity, in gallons, is CLOSEST to

    A. 9,589   B. 13,175   C. 13,274   D. 14,107

14. Assume that a total of 345 people are employed at a certain location.
    If 2/5 of these people report to work at 7:00 A.M. and another 1/5 at 8:00 A.M., then the number of people that have NOT yet reported to work is

    A. 73   B. 138   C. 154   D. 199

15. Assume that a bus consumes an average of 8 gallons of fuel per hour and that each gallon of fuel weighs 7 1/4 pounds.
    In a 6 hour period, the amount of fuel used, in pounds, is

    A. 108   B. 232   C. 348   D. 399

16. The opening Metrocard reading on a daily register is 1,152, and the last Metrocard closing reading is 1,463. The opening cash reading is 12,015, and the last cash closing reading is 24,345. (Reading increases by 30 for each fare.) The total number of revenue-paying passengers that this bus carried on this day is CLOSEST to

    A. 722   B. 1,112   C. 1,463   D. 12,330

17. If it takes a bus 30 seconds to pass two checkpoints that are 500 feet apart, then the speed of the bus is APPROXIMATELY _____ m.p.h.

   A.   10.1   B.   11.4   C.   12.7   D.   14.2

17._____

18. If the length of a particular bus route is 8.6 miles and the average speed of a bus on this route is 7.5 miles per hour, then the one-way running time for a bus is _____ minutes.

   A.   52.3   B.   64.5   C.   68.8   D.   75.6

18._____

19. A certain bus route is five miles long. The schedule speed for half of the route is 6 m.p.h., and for the other half of the route it is 15 m.p.h.
    The AVERAGE schedule speed for the entire route

   A.   is between 6 m.p.h. and 10.5 m.p.h.
   B.   is exactly 10.5 m.p.h.
   C.   is between 10.5 m.p.h. and 15 m.p.h.
   D.   cannot be calculated without knowing running time for each half of the route

19._____

20. A regular tour of duty for an operator requires him to report at 5:50 A.M., leave on his first run at 6:05 A.M., swing from 10:30 A.M. to 2:00 P.M., complete his last run at 5:10 P.M., and clear/at 5:20 P.M. (Notpaid ..for swing time.) The normal pay for this tour is at the operator's regular rate for _____ hours, _____ minutes.

   A.   9; 30   B.   9; 45   C.   10; 15   D.   11; 30

20._____

21. An employee who has a wristwatch which gains 30 minutes per day sets it to the correct time at 6:00 A.M.
    When the watch indicates 12:00 Noon, the CORRECT time, to the nearest minute, is

   A.   11:46   B.   11:53   C.   12:07   D.   12:14

21._____

22. The one-way running time on a bus route is 1 hour and 6 minutes, and the average speed of a bus on this route is 14 m.p.h.
    What is the length, in miles, of this route?

   A.   13.5   B.   14.0   C.   14.4   D.   15.4

22._____

23. A bus consumes 45 gallons of fuel after having traveled a distance of 328 miles.
    The number of miles per gallon of fuel that this bus gets, based on this information, is CLOSEST to

   A.   6.8   B.   7.3   C.   7.8   D.   8.3

23._____

24. A bus operator with a weekday run whose hourly rate of pay is $12.60 normally reports for work at 7:30 A.M. and clears at 3:00 P.M.(On report days he works until 4 P.M.) What is his gross pay for a day on which he is required to write an accident report at the end of his run?

   A. $107.10   B. $108.90   C. $113.40   D. $115.60

24._____

25. A passenger count was made at a certain terminal between 8 A.M. and 9 A.M., and it was noted that eight buses were loaded with the following number of passengers: 34, 52, 29, 63, 19, 17, 56, and 42, respectively.
The TOTAL number of passengers boarding these eight buses was

   A. 302 B. 312 C. 313 D. 412

25.____

KEY (CORRECT ANSWERS)

1. C
2. B
3. C
4. B
5. C

6. C
7. B
8. A
9. D
10. C

11. A
12. B
13. B
14. B
15. C

16. A
17. B
18. C
19. A
20. B

21. B
22. D
23. B
24. A
25. B

SOLUTIONS TO PROBLEMS

1. ($308,645)(.83) ≈ $256,175
2. 220 ft. in 4.9 sec ≈ 45 ft. per sec. Since 60 mph means 88 ft.per sec., the bus is moving at (60)(45/88) ≈ 30 mph
3. .75 - .25 = .50. Then, (3000) (.50/.20) = 7500 miles
4. 40 ft. in 1.5 sec. = 26 2/6 ft. per sec. Thus, the bus is moving at (60)(26 2/3/88) ≈ 18 mph
5. Initial speed is 30 mph = 44 ft. per sec. Final speed (when fully stopped) is 0 ft. per sec. Average speed = 22 ft. per sec. Distance = (average speed)(time) = (22)(10 sec.) = 220 ft.
6. 3 miles in 25 min. means (3)(60/25) = 7.2 ≈ 7 mph
7. Let x = minimum number of married operators under 35 years old. Then, 240-x = number of married operators over 35 years old, and 150-x = number of unmarried operators under 35 years old. Since there are probably operators who are neither married nor under 35 years old, (240-x) + (x) + (150-x) ≤ 300. Solving, x ≥ 90.
8. 5 mph= 1/3; 10 mph= 1/3; 15 mph= 1/3. 5 + 10 + 15= 30. 30 divided by 3= 10 mph average speed.
9. 900,000 ÷ .03 = 30,000,000. Then, 30,000,000 + 900,000 = 30,900,000 ≈ 31,000,000 passengers in August.
10. Terminal B has (300X.85) = 255 operators, so terminal C has (255)(.90) ≈ 230 operators.
11. The scheduled running time for a roundtrip from 11:48 AM to 12:55 PM is 67 minutes. Since the recovery time is 17 minutes (12:55 PM - 1:12 PM), and recovery time must only be deducted once from the running time for a roundtrip, the scheduled running time from terminal to terminal is $\frac{67-17}{2} = \frac{50}{2} = 25$
12. From 10:45 AM to 11:53 AM is 68 minutes. Then, 68 - 6 - 6 = 56 minutes for the scheduled running time.
13. 11,200 ÷ .85 ≈ 13,176, closest to 13,175 gallons
14. (1 - 2/5 - 1/5)(345) = 138 people
15. (6)(8)(7 1/4) = 348 pounds of fuel
16. Number of people paying by Metrocard = 1463 - 1152 = 311 Number of people paying by cash = (24,345-12,015) ÷ 30 = 411 Total of individuals paying revenue = 722
17. 500 ft. in 30 sec. means 16 2/3 ft. per sec. Then, the speed of the bus = (60)(16 2/3 ÷ 88) ≈ 11.4 mph
18. 8.6 ÷ 7.5 = 1.14\overline{6} hrs. = 68.8 min.
19. Times for each half are $\frac{2.5}{6}$ =.41\overline{6} hrs. and $\frac{2.5}{15}$ =.1\overline{6} min. Average speed = 5 ÷ (.41\overline{6} + .1\overline{6}) ≈ 8.6 mph; thus, it is between 6 mph and 10.5 mph.
20. His tour extends from 5:50 AM to 5:20 PM, for a total period of 11 1/2 hours, less swing time from 10:30 AM to 2:00 PM, which is 3 1/2 hours. 11 1/2 - 3 1/2 = 8 hours

21. 30 min/1440 min = .02083̄ gain. Thus, 6 hrs. on the watch indicates

    $6 \div 1.02083\overline{3} \approx 5.88$ hrs. hrs. ≈ 5 hrs. 53 min. in actual time. The actual time is 11:53 AM.

22. Let x = miles on this route. Then, $\dfrac{14}{x} = \dfrac{1 \text{hr.}}{1.10 \text{hrs.}}$ Solving, x = 15.4

23. 328 ÷ 45 ≈ 7.3 miles per gallon

24. 7:30 AM to 4:00 PM = 8 1/2 hrs. Then, ($12.60)(8.5) = $107.10

25. 34 + 52 + 29 + 63 + 19 + 17 + 56 + 42 = 312 passengers

TEST 3

DIRECTIONS: Each question or incomplete statement is followed by several suggested answers or completions. Select the one that BEST answers the question or completes the statement. *PRINT THE LETTER OF THE CORRECT ANSWER IN THE SPACE AT THE RIGHT.*

1. The total automobile traffic of a bridge increased from 33,000 to 37,000. This represents an increase of APPROXIMATELY

    A. 8%   B. 12%   C. 16%   D. 20%

    1.____

2. Eighty percent of the vessels passing under a certain bridge are tugboats. If 105 vessels pass under this bridge daily, the number of tugboats passing under the bridge daily is

    A. 80   B. 84   C. 88   D. 92

    2.____

3. A certain shelf can safely hold 140 pounds. On the shelf is a 45 pound carton of nuts and bolts, a 52 pound carton of assorted hardware, and two containers of lead paint weighing 27 lbs. each.
The shelf

    A. is overloaded by 16 lbs.
    B. can safely hold an additional 16 lbs.
    C. is overloaded by 11 lbs.
    D. can safely hold an additional 11 lbs.

    3.____

4. Of the following decimals, the one which has the same value as 3/8 is

    A. 0.125   B. 0.266   C. 0.333   D. 0.375

    4.____

5. If an iron bar 6'6 1/8" long is cut in half, the length of each piece will then be MOST NEARLY

    A. 3'3 1/16"   B. 3'3 1/8"
    C. 3'6 1/8"   D. 3'6 1/4"

    5.____

6. The amount of liquid that can be stored in 72 one-quart cans is _____ gallons.

    A. 9   B. 18   C. 24   D. 36

    6.____

7. Suppose that an officer carried two packages, one weighing 73 pounds and the other weighing 41 pounds 3 ounces.
The DIFFERENCE between the weights of the two packages was _____ pounds _____ ounces.

    A. 31; 5   B. 31; 13   C. 32; 6   D. 32; 12

    7.____

8. Suppose that the toll money collected at a bridge during March of last year was $153,696.
If the toll money collected at this bridge in April was 3% higher than in March, then the April total was MOST NEARLY

    A. $149,085   B. $158,307   C. $167,431   D. $200,075

    8.____

9. Suppose that 10% more vehicles crossed a certain bridge on Friday than on the previous day.
   If 18,100 cars, 1,290 trucks, and 130 buses used the bridge on Thursday, how many cars, trucks, and buses crossed the bridge on Friday?

   A. 17,568 B. 18,144 C. 19,520 D. 21,472

10. The maximum height allowed for vehicles using a particular bridge under normal conditions is 13 feet 6 inches.
    If a vehicle is 15 feet 5 inches tall, by exactly what amount does the vehicle EXCEED the maximum height limit for this bridge?
    _____ foot(feet) _____ inch(es).

    A. 1; 9 B. 1; 11 C. 2; 1 D. 2; 3

11. The number of cars, trucks, and buses using two different toll lanes on a certain day was as follows:

	Lane 1	Lane 2
Cars	994	1,086
Trucks	113	51
Buses	31	16

    A comparison of these two lanes would show that the TOTAL number of cars, trucks, and buses using Lane 1 on that day was _____ than the total at Lane 2.

    A. 15 fewer B. 25 fewer C. 15 more D. 25 more

12. A certain officer was assigned to collect tolls for two hours. The officer was given $80 in various bills and $150 in quarters so that he could make change. He placed this money in a drawer in the toll booth. At the end of the two hours of toll collecting, the officer had a total of $1,375.75 in the drawer.
    The percent of this total which represents the tolls collected is MOST NEARLY

    A. 15% B. 63% C. 78% D. 83%

13. The number of vehicles using a particular lane each hour during a 6-hour period varied as follows: 134, 210, 213, 234, 111, and 118.
    The AVERAGE number of vehicles per hour using the toll lane during this period was

    A. 150 B. 160 C. 170 D. 180

14. Assume that you have been assigned to a shift which begins at 2:00 P.M., and you want to arrive 10 minutes before the shift begins. If you average 28 miles per hour while driving to work and must travel 21 miles, at exactly what time should you start driving to work?

    A. 12:30 P.M. B. 12:40 P.M.
    C. 1:05 P.M.   D. 1:15 P.M.

15. A rectangular storage room is 15 ft. by 16 ft., and the ceiling height is 10 feet.
    The volume of this room, in cubic feet, is

    A. 2,200 B. 2,300 C. 2,400 D. 2,500

16. One-quarter of the 168 light bulbs on a certain bridge are replaced during the year. If these bulbs cost the city 21 cents each, the yearly cost of replacing the bulbs is

    A. $8.40   B. $8.82   C. $8.86   D. $8.92

    16._____

17. If 14,229 is divided by 17, the answer is

    A. 737   B. 747   C. 837   D. 847

    17._____

18. A worker receives $171.50 per day.
    In 15 working days, his TOTAL earnings should be

    A. $2,560.50   B. $2,562.50
    C. $2,570.50   D. $2,572.50

    18._____

19. If an Assistant Bridge Operator earns $24,500 in the first six months of a year and receives a 10% raise in salary for the next six months of the same year, his total earnings for the year will be

    A. $50,900   B. $51,450   C. $52,750   D. $53,950

    19._____

20. The area of the metal plate shown at the right, minus the hole area, is MOST NEARLY _____ square inches.
    A. 8.5
    B. 8.9
    C. 9.4
    D. 10.1

    20._____

21. The percentage of the tank shown at the right that is filled with water is MOST NEARLY
    A. 33
    B. 35
    C. 37
    D. 39

    21._____

22. Assume that a sump pit measures 10 feet long, 10 feet wide, and 12 feet deep. If each cubic foot of water is equal to 7.5 gallons, the amount of water in the sump when half full will be MOST NEARLY _____ gallons.

    A. 120   B. 1,200   C. 4,500   D. 9,000

    22._____

23. If the water in a sump pit is 10 feet deep, the pressure at the bottom of the pit, in lbs. per sq. in., exerted by the water is MOST NEARLY (assuming water weighs 62.4 lbs./cu. ft.)

    A. 4.3   B. 52   C. 62.4   D. 624

    23._____

24. If part of a walkway measuring 9 feet by 20 feet is to be replaced by concrete 6 inches thick, the cubic yards of concrete needed is MOST NEARLY

    A. 1 1/2   B. 3 1/2   C. 42   D. 90

    24._____

151

25. A new bridge spanning a river is expected to carry 60,000 cars a day on a rainy day and 80,000 cars a day on other kinds of days.
   If there is a $1 toll and one chance in four of a rainy day, the expected value of a day's revenue is

   A. $35,000   B. $75,000   C. $95,000   D. $140,000

25.____

KEY (CORRECT ANSWERS)

1. B
2. B
3. C
4. D
5. A

6. B
7. B
8. B
9. D
10. B

11. A
12. D
13. C
14. C
15. C

16. B
17. C
18. D
19. B
20. B

21. D
22. C
23. A
24. B
25. B

SOLUTIONS TO PROBLEMS

1. $4000 \div 33,000 \approx 12\%$

2. $(105)(.80) = 84$ tugboats

3. $140 - 45 - 52 - (2)(27) = -11$, so the shelf is overloaded by 11 lbs.

4. $3/8 = .375$

5. $(6'6\frac{1}{8}") \div 2 = 3'3\frac{1}{16}"$

6. Since 4 quarts = 1 gallon, 72 quarts = 18 gallons

7. 73 lbs. - 41 lbs. 3 oz. = 31 lbs. 13 oz.

8. $(\$153,696)(1.03) = \$158,307$

9. $(18,100+1,290+130 \times 1.10) = 21,472$ vehicles crossed the bridge on Friday.

10. 15 ft. 5 in. - 13 ft. 6 in. = 1 ft. 11 in.

11. Lane 1 had 1138 vehicles, whereas lane 2 had 1153 vehicles. Lane 1 had 15 fewer vehicles than lane 2.

12. Tolls collected = $\$1375.75 - \$230 = \$1145.75$. Then, $\$1145.75 \div \$1375.75 \approx 83\%$

13. $(134+210+213+234+111+118) \div 6 = 170$ vehicles

14. $21/28 = .75$ hr. Then, 1:50 PM - .75 hr. = 1:05 PM

15. Volume = $(15')(16')(10') = 2400$ cu.ft.

16. Cost = $(.21)(168)(1/4) = \$8.82$

17. $14,229 \div 17 = 837$

18. Total earnings = $(\$171.50)(15) = \$2572.50$

19. Total earnings = $\$24,500 + (1.10)(\$24,500) = \$51,450$

20. $(4)(3) - (\pi)(1)^2 = 8.9$ sq.in.

21. $\dfrac{7"}{18"} \approx 39\%$

22. Half the volume = $(1/2)(10)(10)(12) = 600$ cu.ft.
    Then, $(600)(7.5) = 4500$ gallons

23. Since 1728 cu.in. = 1 cu.ft., 62.4 lbs./cu.ft. = $0.36\overline{1}$ lbs./cu.in. With a depth of 10 ft. or 120 in., pressure = $(.0361 \times 120) \approx 4.3$ lbs./in.^{2}

24. $(9')(20')(1/2') = 90$ cu.ft. $= 90/27 = 3\ 1/3$ or about $3\ 1/2$ cu.yds.

25. $(\$80,000)(.75) + (\$60,000)(.25) = \$75,000$

ARITHMETICAL REASONING
EXAMINATION SECTION
TEST 1

DIRECTIONS: Each question or incomplete statement is followed by several suggested answers or completions. Select the one that BEST answers the question or completes the statement. *PRINT THE LETTER OF THE CORRECT ANSWER IN THE SPACE AT THE RIGHT.*

1. The sum of the fractions 3/32, 3/16, 3/8, and 3/4 is equal to
   A. 1 13/32   B. 1 5/16   C. 1 7/8   D. 3

   1.____

2. If a maintainer earns $11.52 per hour, and time and one-half for overtime, his gross salary for a week in which he works 5 hours over his regular 40 hours should be
   A. $460.80   B. $518.80   C. $547.20   D. $578.80

   2.____

3. If the diameter of a shaft must be 2.620 inches plus or minus .002 inches, the shaft will be SATISFACTORY if it has a diameter of _____ inches.
   A. 2.518   B. 2.600   C. 2.617   D. 2.621

   3.____

4. A bus part costs $275 per 100 when purchased from a vendor. The bus part could be made in the bus machine shop at a labor cost of $60 for 50 units, with material and other costs amounting to $25 for 25 units.
   If 100 such parts were made in the bus shop, there would be a saving of
   A. $55   B. $95   C. $140   D. $165

   4.____

5. The sum of 9/16", 11/32", 15/64", and 1 3/32" is MOST NEARLY
   A. 2.234"   B. 2.134"   C. 2.334"   D. 2.214"

   5.____

6. The diameter of a circle whose circumference is 14.5" is MOST NEARLY
   A. 4.62"   B. 4.81"   C. 4.72"   D. 4.51"

   6.____

7. A bus part cost $90 per 100 when purchased from a vendor. The bus part could be made in the bus machine shop at a labor cost of $20 for 50 units and material and other costs amounting to $10 for 25 units.
   If 100 such parts are made in the bus stop, there would be a saving of
   A. $10   B. $30   C. $40   D. $60

   7.____

8. A bus storage battery having a 300 ampere-hour capacity is 50% discharged. If the bus running schedule for the day is such that the battery will be charging at an average rate of 30 amperes for 2½ hours and discharging at an average rate of 9 amperes for 5 hours, then at the end of the day, the battery will be APPROXIMATELY
   A. at full charge   B. 75% charged
   C. 60% charged   D. 50% charged

   8.____

9. If the total time allowance for replacing the glass in a broken bus window is 75 minutes, how many jobs of this kind would a maintainer be expected to do in 40 hours of work?
   A. 32   B. 40   C. 60   D. 72

10. A certain rod is tapered so that it changes diameter at a rate of ¼ inch per foot of length.
    If the tapered rod is 3 inches long, then the difference in diameter between the two ends is MOST NEARLY
    A. 0.250"   B. 0.187"   C. 0.135"   D. 0.062"

11. How many 9½ inch long pieces of copper tubing can be cut from a 20-foot length of tubing?
    A. 24   B. 25   C. 26   D. 27

12. Two splice plates must be cut from a piece of sheet steel that has an overall length of 14 3/8 inches. The plates are to be 7 5/8 inches and 5 1/4 inches long. If $1/16$ inch is allowed for each saw cut, then how much material would be left?
    A. 1 3/8"   B. 1 1/2"   C. 1 5/8"   D. 1 3/4"

13. A maintainer requires several lengths of tubing for oil lines as follows: $12^{7}/_{16}$ inches, 5/16 inches, 9 3/16 inches, 9 1/8 inches, 6 1/4 inches, and 5 inches. The TOTAL length of tubing required is MOST NEARLY _____ feet.
    A. 2   B. 3   C. 4   D. 5

14. Two-thirds of 10 feet is MOST NEARLY
    A. 6'2"   B. 6'8"   C. 6'11"   D. 7'1"

15. You are directed to pick up a tray load of brake shoes. The combined weight of tray and brake shoes is 4,000 pounds. Assume that each brake shoe weighs 40 pounds and the tray weighs 240 pounds.
    The number of brake shoes in the tray is MOST NEARLY
    A. 88   B. 94   C. 100   D. 106

16. A maintainer earns $37.32 per hour, and time and one-half for overtime over 40 hours. Each week, 15 percent of his total salary is deducted for social security and taxes. Also, each week a $54.00 deduction is made for a savings bond and a $27.00 deduction is made for a charitable organization.
    If he works a total of 46 hours in a week, his take-home pay for that week is
    A. $1,828.50   B. $1,554.30   C. $1,473.38   D. $1,232.10

17. A rectangularly-shaped repair facility for light trucks is 160 feet wide and 260 feet long. A 10-foot space is provided along each wall for benches and equipment. A 60-foot wide area in the middle of the floor is to remain clear for its entire 260 foot length. The entrance to the shop is at one end of this open area.
    Assuming that there are no columns to contend with, the MAXIMUM area available for parking of trucks is _____ sq. ft.
    A. 15,600   B. 19,200   C. 26,000   D. 41,600

3 (#1)

18. A criterion is established that limits the yearly major repair expenses to 30% of the current value of the equipment. Equipment is depreciated at a rate of 20% of its original cost each year. A truck purchased on January 1, 2017 for $27,000 had a reconditioned engine installed in February 2020 at a total cost of $2,700. The amount of money available for additional major repairs on this truck in 2020 is

   A. none B. $540 C. $1,080 D. $2,160

   18.____

19. Twenty carburetors are ordered for your shop by the Purchasing Department. The terms are list, less 30% less 10%, less 5%.
   If the list price of a carburetor is $210 and all terms are met upon delivery, the charges to your budget will be

   A. $4,078.80 B. $3,256.20 C. $2,513.70 D. $1,892.40

   19.____

20. The sum of the fractions 7/16", 11/16", 5/32", and 7/8" is MOST NEARLY
   A. 2.1753" B. 2.1563" C. 1.9522" D. 1.9463"

   20.____

21. If 750 feet of wire weighs 60 lbs., the number of pounds that 150 feet will weigh is MOST NEARLY
   A. 12 B. 10 C. 8 D. 6

   21.____

22. A steel rod 19.750" long is to have three pieces cut from its length. One piece is to be 3.250" long, the second 6.500" long, and the third piece 5.375".
   If .125" is allowed for each cut, the length of the material left over is
   A. 3.750" B. 4.250" C. 4.500" D. 5.150"

   22.____

23. If the distance between the north and south terminals is 10.8 miles and a train makes six roundtrips, then the total mileage would be NEAREST _____ miles.
   A. 22 B. 65 C. 130 D. 145

   23.____

24. If the thickness of material worn from a car wheel is approximately 1/16 inch off the diameter in 20,000 miles of travel, the wheel diameter will be reduced from 33 inches to 32 3/4 inches after _____ miles.
   A. 60,000 B. 80,000 C. 100,000 D. 120,000

   24.____

25. If the distance between north and south terminals is 11.3 miles and a train makes five roundtrips, then the total travel mileage would be NEAREST _____ miles.
   A. 23 B. 55 C. 115 D. 130

   25.____

KEY (CORRECT ANSWERS)

1.	A	11.	B
2.	C	12.	A
3.	D	13.	D
4.	A	14.	B
5.	A	15.	B
6.	A	16.	C
7.	A	17.	B
8.	C	18.	B
9.	A	19.	C
10.	D	20.	B

21. A
22. B
23. C
24. B
25. C

SOLUTIONS TO PROBLEMS

1. $\frac{3}{32} + \frac{3}{16} + \frac{3}{8} + \frac{3}{4} = \frac{45}{32} = 1\frac{13}{32}$

2. Gross salary = ($11.52)(40) + ($17.28)(5) = $547.20

3. 2.620 ± .002 means from 2.618 to 2.622. The only selection in this range is 2.621.

4. ($60)($\frac{100}{50}$) + ($25)($\frac{100}{25}$)$220 if made in the bus shop. Savings = $275 - $220 = $55

5. 9/16" + 11/32" + 15/64" + 1 3/32" = 143/64 = 2 15/64" = 2.234"

6. Diameter = 14.5" ÷ π ≈ 4.62"

7. ($20)($\frac{100}{50}$) + ($10)($\frac{100}{25}$) = $80 if made in the bus shop. Savings = $990 - $80 = $10

8. [150+[(30(2 1/2)] – [(9)(5)] = [150+75] – 45 = 180, and 180/300 = 60%

9. (40)(60) ÷ 75 = 32

10. (1/4")(3/12) = 1/16" ≈ .062"

11. (20)(12) = 240", and 240" ÷ 9 1/2" ≈ 25.3 rounded down to 25 pieces of tubing

12. 14 3/8" − 7 5/8" − 5 1/4" − 1/16" = 1 3/8"

13. 12 7/16" + 14 5/16" + 9 3/16" + 9 1/8" + 6 1/4" + 5" ≈ 5 ft.

14. (2/3)(10') = 6 2/3' = 6'8"

15. 4000 − 240 = 3760 lbs. Then, 3760 ÷ 40 = 94 brake shoes

16. Take-home pay = ($37.32)(40) + ($55.98)(6) − .15[($37.32)(40) + ($55.98)(6)] - $54.00 - $27.00 = $1,473.738 ≈ $1,473.38

17. Subtracting the area for benches and equipment would leave an area of 240' by 140'. Now, deduct the 60' width. Final area = (240')(80') = 19,200 sq.ft.

18. In 2020, the value of the truck = $27,000 − (3)(.20)($27,000) = $10,800. The limit of the expenses for repairs = (.30)($10,800) = $3,240. After installing engine, $3,240 - $2,700 = $540 left for additional major repairs.

19. (20)($210)(.70)(.90)(.95) = $2,513.70

20. 7/16" + 11/16" + 5/32" + 7/8" = 69/32" ≈ 2.1563"

21. (150/750)(60) = 12 lbs.

22. 19.750" − 3.250" − 6.500" − 5.375" - .125" - .125" − 1.25" = 4.250" left over

23. (6)(10.8)(2) = 129.6 ≈ 130 miles

24. 33" − 32 3/4" = 1/4". Then, (1/4 ÷ 1/16)(20,000) = 80,000 miles

25. (5)(11.3)(2) = 113 miles, closest to 115 miles

TEST 2

DIRECTIONS: Each question or incomplete statement is followed by several suggested answers or completions. Select the one that BEST answers the question or completes the statement. *PRINT THE LETTER OF THE CORRECT ANSWER IN THE SPACE AT THE RIGHT.*

1. In looking over an alteration job on car bodies, you find that 96 pieces of 1" × 1" × 1'6" long square steel stock are needed to do this job. Steel weighs 480 lbs. per cu. ft. and costs $0.12 per lb.
   The total cost of this material is MOST NEARLY
   A. $40.00   B. $60.00   C. $80.00   D. $100.00

2. Assume that the breakdown cost of a particular motor job is as follows:
   Parts $160.00
   Labor   75.00
   Overhead   30.00
   The percentage of the total cost for labor is MOST NEARLY
   A. 20%   B. 25%   C. 28%   D. 32%

3. The engine hydraulic system and transmission on a certain type of tractor use the same type oil. This oil is delivered in 55 gallon drums.
   How many drums are needed to make all three changes on 10 of these tractors whose capacities are the following:
   Engine   58 quarts
   Transmission   70 quarts
   Hydraulic system 22 gallons
   A. 100   B. 50   C. 54   D. 10

4. A new shop layout requires the following:
   1,000 sq. ft. for tool room
   3,000 sq. ft. for parts room
   10,000 sq. ft. for service bays
   5,500 sq. ft. for isles
   The building should be AT LEAST _____ yards wide and 70 yards long.
   A. 10   B. 20   C. 25   D. 30

5. When filling a diesel engine cooling system, the mix required is 80% antifreeze and 20% water. You are required to fill seven systems containing 30 gallons each. The number of 5 gallon cans of antifreeze that are required is MOST NEARLY
   A. 210   B. 168   C. 34   D. 26

6. The floors of 2 cars are to be painted with a special test paint. Assume that the floor area in each car is 600 square feet. A gallon of this paint will cover 400 square feet.
   The number of gallons of this paint that you should pick up at the storeroom to paint the two car floors would be
   A. 6   B. 5   C. 4   D. 3

7. Assume that you are sent to the storeroom for 1,000 of 600-volt contact tips which are to be distributed equally to 5 foremen, but you find that the storeroom can only supply you with 825.
If you distribute these 825 tips equally to the 5 foremen the number of tips that each foreman will receive is
A. 165   B. 175   C. 190   D. 200

8. You are asked to fill six 5-gallon cans of oil from a full drum containing 52 gallons. When you have filled the six cans, the number of gallons of oil left in the drum will be MOST NEARLY
A. 14   B. 16   C. 22   D. 30

9. A certain wire rope is made up of 6 strands, each strand containing 19 wires. The TOTAL number of wires in this wire rope is
A. 25   B. 96   C. 114   D. 144

10. The hook should be the weakest part of any crane, hoist, or sling.
According to this statement, if a particular hook has a rated capacity of 2½ tons, then the MAXIMUM load that should be lifted with this hook is _____ pounds.
A. 150   B. 3,000   C. 5,000   D. 5,500

11. Assume that 2 car wheels weigh 635 pounds each and are attached to an axle weighing 1,260 pounds.
The total weight of this assembly is MOST NEARLY _____ pounds.
A. 1,270   B. 1,520   C. 1,895   D. 2,530

12. If an employee authorizes his employer to deduct 4% of his $1,200 weekly salary for a savings bond, the MINIMUM number of weekly deductions required to get enough money to buy a bond costing $144 is
A. 3   B. 6   C. 8   D. 9

13. In weighing out a truckful of scrap metal, the scale reads 21,496 lbs.
If the empty truck weighs 9,879 lbs., the amount of scrap metal, in pounds, is MOST NEARLY
A. 10,507   B. 10,602   C. 11,617   D. 12,617

14. Four trays of material are placed on the body of a delivery truck for delivery to the inspection shop. Each tray is 4 feet wide and 4 feet long.
If these trays are placed side by side on the floor of the delivery truck, together they will cover an area of the floor MOST NEARLY _____ square feet.
A. 32   B. 48   C. 64   D. 72

15. Assume that you are operating a degreasing tank and its tray holds 5 gear cases. It takes 40 minutes to clean one tray of gear cases.
At the end of 6 hours of operation (excluding lunch break and loading and unloading time), the number of gear case cleaned will be
A. 30   B. 36   C. 45   D. 50

16. If a serviceman's weekly gross salary is $160 and 20% is deducted for taxes, his take-home pay is
    A. $120   B. $128   C. $140   D. $144

Questions 17-18.

DIRECTIONS: Questions 17 and 18 are to be answered on the basis of the following paragraph.

The car maintenance department is considering the purchase of a certain car part from Manufacturer X for $140. An equivalent part can be purchased from Manufacturer Y for $100. The part made by Manufacturer X must be reconditioned every 3 years, using material costing $30 and requiring 6 hours of labor. The part made by Manufacturer Y must be reconditioned every 1½ years, using material costing $24 and requiring 5 hours of labor. The maintainer's rate of pay is $12 per hour.

17. The cost of operating with the part made by Manufacturer X (excluding the first cost) is MOST NEARLY _____ per year.
    A. $30   B. $32   C. $34   D. $42

18. The total cost of operating with the part made by Manufacturer Y over a period of 12 years, including the first cost of the part and assuming the part is scrapped at the end of 12 years, is MOST NEARLY
    A. $472   B. $572   C. $688   D. $772

19. The area of the steel plate shown in the sketch at the right is _____ sq. ft.
    A. 16
    B. 18
    C. 20
    D. 22

20. A car part made by a Manufacturer X has a purchase cost of $7,500 and a life of 5 years. It requires a yearly maintenance cost of $50. Manufacturer Y offers a similar part of this type for $4,800, with a life of 3 years and a yearly maintenance cost of $75.
    By purchasing the part offering a better overall value, the yearly savings per unit purchased would be
    A. $115   B. $125   C. $135   D. $140

21. A car part can be overhauled at the rate of 12 parts per hour. Each part requires new material costing $6 each.
    If the labor cost is $14 per hour, one part can be overhauled for a total cost (labor plus material) of MOST NEARLY
    A. $6.64   B. $7.16   C. $7.46   D. $8.20

4 (#2)

22. A car part costs $150 per 50 units when purchased in a finished condition from a vendor. The car part can be made in the shop at a total cost off $2.20 per unit, when made on a machine which can be purchased for $1,000.
The MINIMUM number of parts which must be made on this machine before the savings equal the cost of the machine is
A. 850   B. 1,000   C. 1,250   D. 1,500

22._____

23. A pound of a certain type of metal washer contains 360 washers.
If ¼ of the material of each washer is removed by enlarging the center of each washer, the number of washers to the pound should then be MOST NEARLY
A. 280   B. 300   C. 380   D. 480

23._____

24. A maintainer earns $32.52 per hour, and time and one-half for overtime. Ten percent of his total salary earned is deducted from his paycheck for social security and taxes. He also contributes $15.00 per week to a charitable organization. No other deductions are made.
If he works 2 hours over his basic 40 hours, his weekly take-home pay should be MOST NEARLY
A. $1,398.36   B. $1,258.50   C. $1,243.50   D. $1,231.80

24._____

25. A car part costs $130 per 100 units if purchased from a vendor. The car part can be made on a machine which can be purchased for $1,000. Assume that this machine has a production life of 20,000 units with no salvage value, and that all shop costs amount to $80 per 100 units turned out in the shop.
The money that would be SAVED during the life of the machine would be
A. $800   B. $8,000   C. 9,000   D. $18,000

25._____

KEY (CORRECT ANSWERS)

1. B
2. C
3. D
4. D
5. C

6. D
7. A
8. C
9. C
10. C

11. D
12. A
13. C
14. C
15. C

16. B
17. C
18. C
19. C
20. B

21. B
22. C
23. D
24. C
25. C

SOLUTIONS TO PROBLEMS

1. Total cost ≈ (96)(.01)(4)(.12) ≈ $55, which is closest to $60. Note that 1" × 1" × 1'6" ≈ (1/12')(1/12')(3/2') – 1.96 ≈ .01 cu. ft.

2. Labor = $75 ÷ $265 ≈ 28%

3. (10)(14.5+17.5+22) = 540. Then, 540 ÷ 55 ≈ 10 drums

4. Total sq. ft. = 19,500, which is 2166 2/3 sq. yds. Then, 2166 2/3 ÷ 70 ≈ 30.95 or 31

5. Amount of antifreeze = (.80)(7)(.30) = 168 gallons. Then, 168 ÷ 5 ≈ 34 cans

6. (600+600) ÷ 400 = 3 gallons

7. 825 ÷ 5 = 165 for each foreman

8. 52 – (6)(5) = 22 gallons left

9. (19)(6) = 114 wires

10. (2½)(2000) = 5000 pounds

11. (2)(635) + 1260 = 2530 pounds

12. ($1,200)(.04) = $48. Then, $144 ÷ $48 = 3 weekly deductions

13. 21,496 – 9,879 = 11,617 pounds

14. 4(4')(4') = 64 sq. ft.

15. 6 hrs. ÷ 2/3 hr. = 9 trays = 45 gear cases cleaned

16. Take-home pay = ($160)(.80) = $128

17. ($30)+(6)($12) = ($102 for 3 yrs. = $34 per year

18. 100 + 7(24) + 7(60) = 688

19. Separate the figure into regions as follows:
    I: 1'×2' = 2 sq.ft.
    II: 3'×4' = 12 sq.ft.
    III: (3'×4') ÷ 2' = 6 sq.ft.
    Total = 20 sq.ft.

    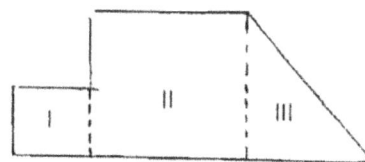

20. Manufacturer X: $7500 + ($50)(5) = $7750, so the cost per year is $7750 ÷ 5 = $1550
    Manufacturer Y: $4800 + (3)($75) = $5025, so the cost per year is $5025 ÷ 3 = $1675
    Using Manufacturer X, savings = $125 per year

21. Cost of 12 parts = (12)($6) + $14 = $86. Then, the cost of one part = $86 ÷ 12 ≈ $7.16.2021

22. Savings per unit is $150/50 - $2.20 = $.80. Then, $1000 ÷ $.80 = 1250

23. 1 – ¼ = ¾. Then, 360 ÷ 34 = 480

24. Take-home pay = [($32.52)(40)+($48.78)(2)][.90] - $15 ≈ $1,243.50

25. Amount if purchased from a vendor = $130(200) = $26,000. Using the machine, amount = $1000 + ($80)(200) = $17,000. Amount saved = $9000

TEST 3

DIRECTIONS: Each question or incomplete statement is followed by several suggested answers or completions. Select the one that BEST answers the question or completes the statement. *PRINT THE LETTER OF THE CORRECT ANSWER IN THE SPACE AT THE RIGHT.*

1. A Cat 983 Traxcavator can make a complete loading cycle from bank to truck and back to bank in 25 seconds.
   If the bucket contains 4 cu. yds of loose material, the MINIMUM amount of material that an operator should load in 4 hours is _____ cubic yards.
   A. 2,304　　B. 2,100　　C. 1,896　　D. 576

   1.____

2. An excavation is 12' × 18' × 15' and is to be dug by a Cat 983 Traxcavator with 3 cubic yards of solid material excavated per pass.
   The MINIMUM number of passes required to dig the hole is _____ passes.
   A. 40　　B. 46　　C. 120　　D. 126

   2.____

3. A Cat D8 tractor and 463 scraper can haul 22 cubic yards of cover material per trip.
   If it is required to cover an area 1,000 feet by 100 feet to a depth of 2 feet, the MINIMUM number of trips that will be required is MOST NEARLY
   A. 284　　B. 337　　C. 385　　D. 421

   3.____

4. Gravel weighs 2,800 pounds per cubic yard.
   In order to carry 42,000 pounds of gravel, the capacity of a truck must be AT LEAST _____ cubic yards.
   A. 10　　B. 12　　C. 15　　D. 18

   4.____

5. The average capacity of an Athey Wagon is 60 cubic yards. The Cat D8 tractor pulls 2 wagons.
   The MINIMUM number of trips to the fill that would be required to empty a barge loaded with 1,000 cubic yards of refuse is
   A. 9　　B. 17　　C. 30　　D. 90

   5.____

6. When pulling 2 Athey trailers, the operator of a Cat D8 tractor can make a round trip from the crane to the fill and back in 15 minutes.
   Assuming that delays and breaks allow the man to work productively for 75% of the shift, the MAXIMUM number of trips that the operator can make in an 8-hour shift is
   A. 43　　B. 32　　C. 24　　D. 16

   6.____

7. In plowing a street which is 24 feet wide, a motor grader can make an 8-ft. wide pass, with a 2-ft. overlap.
   If a roundtrip takes 4 minutes, the MINIMUM time needed to plow this street should be _____ minutes.
   A. 12　　B. 16　　C. 24　　D. 32

   7.____

8. A scraper is loaded with 23 cubic yards of sand weighing 100 pounds per cubic foot.
   The weight of the load, in tons, is MOST NEARLY
   A. 20 B. 30 C. 40 D. 60

9. Assume a crankcase oil change of 6 quarts for every 150 service hours.
   How many 42 gallon drums of oil are required for 8,400 total service hours.
   A. 5 B. 2 C. 1 D. 1 1/3

10. Assume that a ruler is marked in 10ths of a foot instead of in inches.
    5 tenths on this ruler would be
    A. 4" B. 5" C. 6" D. 7"

11. A truckload of 1½" stone from a 10 cubic yard truck will spread an area APPROXIMATELY _____ long, 6" deep, and _____ wide.
    A. 50'; 10' B. 10';5' C. 54';10' D. 45'; 5'

12. A dump truck with a body 10 ft. long, 5 ft. wide, and 4 ft. deep has a volume of _____ cubic feet.
    A. 150 B. 200 C. 250 D. 300

13. A tractor is operated on a given landfill operation during the following time intervals in one day: from 8:15 A.M. to 11:45 A.M.; from 12:30 P.M. to 6:00 P.M.; from 6:45 P.M. to 11:30 P.M.
    The total net operating time, expressed in hours and minutes, is MOST NEARLY
    A. 13; 30 B. 13; 15 C. 13; 45 D. 12; 45

14. The area of ground contact (with standard track shoes) of a late model D8 Caterpillar Tractor is 4,296 sq. in.
    Expressed in square feet, this is MOST NEARLY
    A. 358 B. 29.8 C. 159.3 D. 21.37

15. A towing winch develops a bare drum line pull of 11.8 tons.
    This force represents, in pounds,
    A. 23,850 B. 28,300 C. 23,800 D. 23,600

16. The fuel tank gauge reads about ¾ of a full tank.
    If the tank capacity is 72.5 gallons, the amount of fuel in the tank is MOST NEARLY
    A. 53.2 B. 53.8 C. 54.5 D. 55.0

17. If a dump truck capable of carrying 40 2/3 cubic yards is ¾ loaded, it is carrying, in cubic yards,
    A. 28 B. 36½ C. 30½ D. 28 2/3

18. A load of sand filling a truck body 6 feet long, 5 feet wide, and 3 feet deep would contain _____ cubic feet.
    A. 14 B. 90 C. 33 D. 21

Questions 19-21.

DIRECTIONS: Questions 19 through 21 are to be answered on the basis of the diagrams of balanced levers shown below. P is the center of rotation, W is the weight on the lever, and F is the balancing force.

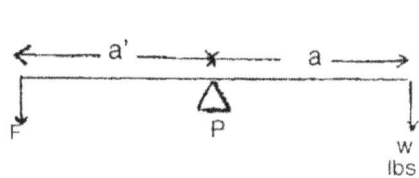
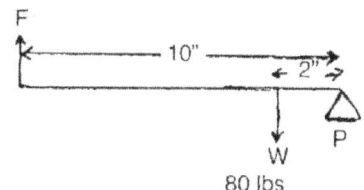

19. In Diagram 1, the force F required to balance the weight W lbs. on the lever shown is equal to _____ lbs.
    A. a/W   B. W/a   C. W   D. Wa

    19.____

20. In Diagram 2, the force F required to balance the weight of 80 lbs. on the lever shown is _____ lbs.
    A. 4   B. 3   C. 16   D. 32

    20.____

21. The mechanical advantage of the lever shown in Diagram 2 is
    A. 4   B. 5   C. 8   D. 12

    21.____

22. The specific gravity of a liquid may be defined as the ratio of the weight of a given volume of the liquid to the weight of an equal volume of water. An empty bottle weighs 5 oz. When the bottle is filled with water, the total weight is 50 oz. When the bottle is filled with another liquid, the total weight is 95 oz. The specific gravity of the second liquid is MOST NEARLY
    A. .50   B. .58   C. 1.7   D. 2.0

    22.____

23. If one inch is approximately equal to 2.54 centimeters, the number of inches in one meter is MOST NEARLY
    A. 14.2   B. 25.4   C. 39.4   D. 91.4

    23.____

24. One-quarter divided by five-eighths is
    A. 5/32   B. 1/10   C. 2/5   D. 5/2

    24.____

25. A man works on a certain job continuously, with no time off for lunch. If he works from 9:45 A.M. until 1:35 P.M. to finish the job, the total time which he spent on the job is MOST NEARLY _____ hours, _____ minutes.
    A. 3; 10   B. 3; 35   C. 3; 50   D. 4; 15

    25.____

KEY (CORRECT ANSWERS)

1.	A		11.	C
2.	A		12.	B
3.	B		13.	C
4.	C		14.	B
5.	A		15.	D
6.	C		16.	C
7.	B		17.	C
8.	B		18.	B
9.	B		19.	C
10.	C		20.	C

21. B
22. D
23. C
24. C
25. C

SOLUTIONS TO PROBLEMS

1. 4 hrs. = (4)(60)(60) = 14,400 sec. Then, 14,400 ÷ 25 = 576. Thus, (576)(4 cu.yds.) = 2304

2. (12')(18')(15') = 3240 cu.ft. = 120 cu.yds. Then, 120 ÷ 3 = 40

3. (1000')(100')(2') = 200,000 cu.ft. ≈ 7407.4 cu.yds. Finally, 7407.4 ÷ 22 = 336.7, rounded up to 337 trips

4. 42,000 ÷ 2800 = 15 cu.yds.

5. (2)(60 cu.yds.) = 120 yds. Then, 1000 ÷ 120 = 8 1/3, which must be rounded up to 9 trips.

6. 8 hrs. ÷ 15 min. = 32. Then, (32)(.75) = 24 trips

7. 24' ÷ 8' = 3; however, with a 2 ft. overlap, only 6' gets plowed. So, (24÷6)(4 min) = 16 min.

8. 23 cu.yds = 621 cu.ft. Then, (621)(100) = 62,100 lbs. Finally, 62,100 ÷ 2000 ≈ 30 tons

9. 8400 ÷ 150 = 56. Then, (56)(6 qts.) = 336 qts. = 8 gallons. Finally, 84 ÷ 42 = 2 drums

10. 5 tenths = (5/10)(12") = 6"

11. (54')(1/2')(10') = 270 cu.ft. = 10 cu.yds.

12. Volume = (10')(5')(4') = 200 cu.ft.

13. 3 hrs. 30 min. + 5 hrs. 30 min. + 4 hrs. 45 min. = 12 hrs. 105 min. = 13 hrs. 45 min.

14. 4296 sq.in. = 4296 ÷ 144 ≈ 29.8 sq.ft.

15. 11.8 tons = (11.8)(2000) = 23,600 lbs.

16. (72.5)(.75) = 54.375, closest to 54.5 gallons

17. (40 2/3)(3/4) = 30½ cu.yds.

18. (6')(5')(3') = 90 cu.ft.

19. $F = Wa/a = W$ lbs.

20. F = (80)(2) ÷ 10 = 16 lbs.

21. Mechanical advantage = 10/2 = 5

22. Specific gravity = $\frac{95-5}{50-5}$ = 2

23. 1 meter = 100 cm. ≈ (100) ÷ (2.54) ≈ 39.4 in.

24. $1/4 \div 5/8 = \dfrac{1}{4} \cdot \dfrac{8}{5} = \dfrac{2}{5}$

25. 9:45 A.M. to 1:35 P.M. = 3 hrs. 50 min.

www.ingramcontent.com/pod-product-compliance
Lightning Source LLC
Chambersburg PA
CBHW082042300426
44117CB00015B/2571